LEMONADE PICKLES & WORMS

The Many Faces of Transition

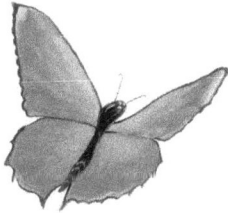

WHAT THEY'RE SAYING ABOUT
LEMONADE, PICKLES & WORMS,
THE MANY FACES OF TRANSITION

"This book will change your life! Jamie Wagner is one of those rare individuals gifted with the ability, tenacity and insight to truly bring each reader the power tools to understand and move through transition with ease, grace, and even fun!"

~ Mary Morrissey, speaker and author
Online at www.marymorrissey.com

"Fantastic! Fun! Life-transforming! A great book that helps support all of us in transition on our life's journey."

~ Dr. Judy Ellison, Ph.D., psychologist, author and speaker

"These days it seems as if there is a lot to entertain us, and a lot to inspire us in the self-help arena. However, it is a beautiful and magical thing when entertainment and inspiration show up in one package! *Lemonade, Pickles & Worms* is a book with charming real life stories that inspire on their own. Yet, there are profoundly inspirational ideas for living life to its fullest and powerful questions to invite us into new ways of approaching life. It is truly a delightful adventure!"

~ Rev. Dr. Michelle Medrano, Community Spiritual Leader
New Vision Center for Spiritual Living, Phoenix, AZ

"Join Jamie as she recaptures her own original essence, hidden in the memories of childhood — and in the process of this journey, come alive to who *you* have *really* been all along."

~ David Robert Ord, Author: *Your Forgotten Self* and *Lessons in Loving — A Journey into the Heart*, Namaste Publishing

"What a gift! I love this book. It weaves so many important ideas, life lessons, and personal growth concepts within the context of a true life story."

~ Carol Gates, author of *As You Wish*
and President of Bob Proctor Coaching Program

"Jamie gives us life lessons in a delightfully digestible way. Her stories are great metaphors as well as fun reading. I could see myself in almost every page."

~ **Marcia Reynolds, Psy.D., author of** *Outsmart Your Brain:*
How to Make Success Feel Easy

"This book offers a road map to help break free from what holds us back in life's transitions. *Lemonade, Pickles & Worms* is an inspiring read that can help you change."

~**Andrew Erlich, Ph.D., author of** *Exploring Culture:*
How to Do Business with 17 Different Cultural Groups **and**
The Long Shadows **(2010)**

"In *Lemonade, Pickles & Worms,* Jamie Wagner shows you how to get a powerful return on the investment of time and energy in exploring the essence of you. The ageless principles and sweet, personal examples set forth in this book will guide you in getting reacquainted with your inner child in a whole new way. When you stop, look and listen using Jamie's wise approach, you literally transform your life!"

~ **Rev. Karen Russo, MBA, award-winning author,** *The Money Keys:*
Unlocking Peace, Freedom and Real Financial Power

"What a journey down our past with a template for life success and handling pain. A lesson and awakening guideline at the turn of each chapter. Jamie grabs you and doesn't let you go. Enjoy!"

~ **Bill Johnson, CSP, National Sales Manager FORTUNE 500 Ampex**
Corporation, First Executive Vice President,
National Speakers Association

"*Lemonade, Pickles & Worms* is a must read for those who want to let go of cultural norms and early childhood experiences that prevent them from "being" their authentic self. Jamie so eloquently reminds us that life seen through rose-colored glasses is actually the real life we were meant to live. It's these glasses that allow us to truly embrace life, change, and transition and see the magnificent unfolding of our own purpose and spirit in the process. Reading this book provides a road map to bring you closer to finding your own "buried treasure" of self. Wonderful!"

~ **Dr. Wendy Nickerson, Psy.D., psychologist, life coach,**
author, inspirational speaker

"This book is beautifully written by an inspired author and entrepreneur. It will influence the way people think about their lives, because Jamie wrote from experience and her heart. I am proud to have known such an eloquent writer."

~ **Patricia Noel Drain, CPC, CSP, author, professional speaker**

"*Lemonade, Pickles & Worms* is a delicious feast for the mind, heart and soul! Jamie Wagner shares the ultimate step-by-step recipe for embracing transition and living your most fulfilling life, using the ingredients *you* have buried in your mental and emotional cupboards! It's time to cook up and savor the life that you want and deserve!"

~ **Top Dog Eileen Proctor, Pet Lifestyle and Industry Expert**

"I loved this book! *Lemonade, Pickles & Worms* is not only a great read but also the observations and life's principles exemplified in Jamie Wagner's personal journey are relatable to anyone trying to make sense out of unplanned detours. This book teaches that transitions in life are just a part of the journey and that change is something to embrace, not fear, regardless of how uncomfortable one may feel at the time."

~ **Peter J. Burns, III, Entrepreneur: started over 100 companies, a Dean at Andrew Jackson University, founded Club E Network and Young Entrepreneurs Organization**

LEMONADE
PICKLES &
WORMS *The Many Faces of Transition*

Jamie Wagner

with **Bill Wagner**

LEMONADE, PICKLES & WORMS

Copyright 2010, All Rights Reserved
Jamie and Bill Wagner
Scottsdale, Arizona

ISBN 13: 978-0-9840585-0-1

Library of Congress Catalog Number 2009928295

E-Mail: *Info@TuckerTaleProductions.com*
Web Site URL: *http://www.TuckerTaleProductions.com*

Tucker Tale Productions, Publisher

Printed in the United States of America

DEDICATION

To my loving husband, best friend and life partner, Bill.
Thank you for always being there for me with your love,
understanding, and commitment!

To my loving dogs Tucker & Taylor.
Thank you for the unconditional love you give!

In remembrance of my loving parents.
Thank you for sharing your values, love, guidance, confidence,
and allowing me such independence as a child!

To my sister, Lindy,
my brother, Bill
and my sister-in-law, Bonnie.
Thank you all for your love, loyal support and friendship!

And finally, a special tribute to all those who would find value
and wisdom contained herein.
It is my sincerest wish your life be enhanced
with joy, peace of mind, and continuous fulfillment!

CONTENTS

CONTENTS

CONTENTS

CONTENTS

CONTENTS

ACKNOWLEDGMENTS

Producing a book is an arduous, time consuming and creatively exhausting undertaking. I have found that the initial creation and development of a manuscript is only the beginning of the myriad tasks and talents required to bring a written work to print. Therefore, it is my pleasure and profound privilege to acknowledge and honor those who have literally made this book possible.

First a big, warm, loving "Thank you!" to my husband and co-author, Bill Wagner, whose ability to bring my creative desires to life through his expressive application of the written word was vital to this book.

My sincerest thanks to dear friend, published author and literary analyst extraordinaire David Robert Ord, for forwarding and capturing the soul of this book as only he could.

An earnest thanks to Paul McNeese for his editorial services. A big "high five" to talented and award winning book cover and graphic designer Hoi Yan Patrick Cheung for his innovative, creative and artistic expertise and agreeing to adorn our front cover with a Patrick Cheung original painting. An additional thanks to the imaginative touch of Jenny Campbell and her intuitive and creative illustrative expertise.

Our heartfelt appreciation to all those who contributed to the *"Faces of Transition"* chapter and consented to share some of their most private and intimate transformational experiences.

To Jeanne Mac Laughlin and Barbara Horton of the singing group "The JaJa's" for contributing the lyrics from their song "Just Like A Child," and to Curt Yeager for allowing us to include his poem, "Prison." A special thanks to our photographer, Jorgen, of "Fotos by Jorgen," for his innate ability to capture one's soul in a simple photograph.

And finally, an appreciative thank you to all those friends and unnamed (but no less significant) supporters who provided us with the encouragement and kick-butt impetus to stay the course.

SPECIAL THANKS

A heartfelt thanks to all the inspirational teachers, mentors and personal development gurus who have guided me and inspired me to reach for the stars and to take ownership of this wonderful gift called "life!" My sincerest gratitude to:

REV. DR. MICHAEL BECKWITH, Founder of the Agape International Spiritual Center, teacher, and author

GREGG BRADEN, Author, pioneer in bridging science and spirituality

MICHAEL BROWN, Author of *The Presence Process* and *Alchemy of the Heart*

MRS. CAMPBELL, My third grade teacher; a lady who believed in me!

JACK CANFIELD, Inspirational best selling author, success coach

THE DALAI LAMA, Spiritual leader of the Tibetan people

DR. DEEPAK CHOPRA, Mind-body spirit guru, author

DR. WAYNE DYER, Self-help author, inspirational teacher, speaker

GERALDINE EFREMOFF, Junior high school teacher; took me to the next level

T. HARV EKER, Author, motivational speaker, trainer

EDWENE GAINES, Abundant consciousness teacher, author

LOUISE HAY, Metaphysical lecturer, international best-selling author

ESTHER AND JERRY HICKS, Authors and speakers

NAPOLEON HILL, Self-improvement author

ERNEST HOLMES, Author, founder of the worldwide Religious Science movement

LORAL LANGEMEIER, Financial author, strategist, wealth consultant

REV. KATHRYN MCDOWELL, Spiritual educator and minister

OG MANDINO, Best-selling inspirational author

REV. DR. MICHELLE MEDRANO, Inspirational minister, teacher

MARY MORRISSEY, Teacher, author, counselor and minister

EARL NIGHTINGALE, Self-improvement pioneer

JOEL OSTEEN, Inspirational minister, author

BOB PROCTOR, Personal development trainer, author, speaker, coach

ANTHONY ROBBINS, Motivational expert, author, coach

DON MIGUEL RUIZ, Author, teacher

ECKHART TOLLE, Contemporary spiritual teacher, author

BRIAN TRACY, Self-development and motivational author, speaker

DOREEN VIRTUE, Spiritual doctor of psychology, author, speaker

DENIS WAITLEY, Productivity consultant, author, speaker

WALLACE D. WATTLES, Turn-of-the-century author

PHILLIP WHALEY, Junior high school teacher; a true teacher, full of heartfelt caring

MARIANNE WILLIAMSON, Author, lecturer

OPRAH WINFREY, Inspirational talk show host, author, philanthropist

ZIG ZIGLAR, Self-help author, inspirational speaker

And last but not least, my seven canine collaborators: Shana, Sherman, Bauser, Jasmine, Tyler, and of course, Tucker and Taylor.

The purpose of our lives is to be happy.

~ Dalai Lama

*We plan our lives according to a dream
that came to us in our childhood, and we find
that life alters our plans.
And yet, at the end, from a rare height,
we also see that our dream was our fate.
It's just that providence had other ideas
as to how we would get there.
Destiny plans a different route,
or turns the dream around, as if it were a riddle,
and fulfills the dream in ways we couldn't have expected.*

~ Ben Okri

*You are never given a wish without also being given
the power to make it come true.*

~ Richard Bach

*What we call the secret of happiness
is no more than our willingness to choose life.*

~ Leo Buscaglia

Whenever a door closes, a new one always opens.

~ Helen Keller

*Dreams are renewable. No matter what our age or condition, there are still
untapped possibilities within us and new beauty
waiting to be born.*

~ Dr. Dale Turner

FOREWORD

We live in an age when there's tremendous interest in self-improvement. It's a luxury most of the generations that have gone before us never enjoyed because practically their entire lives were spent in the hard labor of simply surviving, raising families, and, in most cases, dying before they ever had the chance to experience a midlife crisis.

Browse the shelves of your local bookstore and you'll see that self-help books abound. There's advice on how to improve just about any area of life—advice that comes from all sorts of different angles, some of which clash. We're told we ought to do it "this way," but just when we find that approach isn't working, along comes another author and says, "No, that was the wrong way. My way is far better."

Many of you reading this book have already tried countless approaches to making your life more meaningful, more fulfilling. So why should you read this book? What's different about it?

Well, in one sense, *Lemonade, Pickles & Worms* is about self-improvement in that it will certainly enable you to improve your life. But as you read what Jamie Wagner has shared of her own journey, you'll realize there's something crucially different between the plethora of self-help techniques currently available and what *Lemonade, Pickles & Worms* invites us to do.

The difference lies in the fact there's no *method* we have to learn and then try to put into practice. Instead of giving us a formula, what Jamie asks of us is to allow who we have always really been, and what we have known from very early on in life, to surface within us.

If you've had the luxury of a midlife crisis or are in one now, count yourself blessed. The crisis you are experiencing isn't something alien to you, being thrust on you unsolicited by the circumstances you find yourself in. Rather, it's emerging from your *own deepest being* — a part of you that you're perhaps not accustomed to experiencing.

Neither is what you are going through something that's trying to destroy what happiness you may have enjoyed. Whether it takes the form of a divorce, ill health, a financial reversal, or some other seeming tragedy, such a time in our lives is in reality a moment of *grace*.

During this moment, an aspect of ourselves we are unacquainted with is seeking to break into our everyday reality. It's actually the most important part of us, our authentic being. But it feels strange to us, even hostile — as if it were out to sabotage us — because although we once lived from what now seeks to arise in us, there was a time long ago when we lost touch with this core of ourselves pretty much altogether.

The author doesn't offer us a *method*, because what *Lemonade, Pickles & Worms* asks of us isn't about something we have to *do*. It's about someone we have to *be* — our original, precious self. All we are asked to do is allow what is happening at any given moment in our life to be our teacher, so that it has an opportunity to bring to our attention what we have always sensed about ourselves, always really known.

When we are in touch with the aspect of ourselves *Lemonade, Pickles & Worms* invites us to discover, we no longer need someone to show us the way, hold our hand, and validate us. We no longer have any difficulty at all discerning the right path for our life. All the guidance we need for every situation we could ever face flows spontaneously from within us, precisely when we need it — coupled with the wisdom and strength to carry out what needs to be done.

Join Jamie as she recaptures her own original essence, hidden in the memories of childhood — and in the process of this journey, come alive to who *you* have *really* been all along.

~ David Robert Ord
Author: *Your Forgotten Self* and *Lessons in Loving — A Journey into the Heart*, Namaste Publishing

CHILD'S PLAY

Reading between the lines

Between a few of the chapters, I have included some recollections as seen through my eyes as a child, called **"Child's Play."** These personal childhood narratives were meant to illustrate how our experiential perceptions as children ultimately impact our life as adults, and why seemingly trivial childhood events can program our subconscious with positive or negative emotional charges that we carry into adulthood.

These five short stories have been set in the type face you are reading and spread throughout the book in columns somewhat narrower than the main text so as to clearly differentiate between my recollections of yesterday and my reality today.

INTRODUCTION

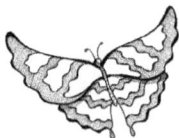

"Is that me?" you find yourself asking. You're gazing into the bathroom mirror, just as you've done almost every morning of your life. Yet . . . this time you seem to sense something profoundly different. There's something in and behind those baby blues you haven't noticed before—something disconcerting, very curious, yet exciting at the same time. You begin to feel as though you're looking at a total stranger!

"Well, at long last it's happened," you muse. "I've finally lost my mind!"

It's true, you might be feeling a little frustrated and you may be in a temporary state of confusion, but hold off on that call to the funny farm. Millions of evolving adults have gone through, are presently going through, or will eventually go through this phenomenon at some time in their lives. You may not find that reflection in the bathroom mirror as familiar as it once was, simply because it's not you anymore. It's not who you were, definitely not who you are, and maybe not even someone you may become.

What you're looking at is the face of transition!

What you see are eyes full of life, love, wonder and—yes—a healthy dose of apprehension, too. In that split second you feel something has ended, but you also have a sense of a new beginning. You suddenly realize it's only half-time. The game is far from over. "So now what?" you ask yourself. "Could it be I have only just begun? What do I want to do with the rest of my life? For what do I really want to trade the rest of my days?"

I wrote this book because I've had the same life-changing experience.

Like so many people before me, I found myself staring blankly into the unforgiving face of transition.

At that moment, time appeared to stand still. I knew it was time to stop my world and get off at the next station. I needed to think, ponder, reflect and take whatever time I needed to seriously plan the rest of my life. But alas, I ignored this life-saving revelation. I blindly reasoned I didn't have the time to take the time. I had bills to pay, as well as obligations to friends, family and business associates. I couldn't afford to interrupt my life in order to consider the rest of it, or so I thought. I mistakenly reasoned, "This is not the right time" . . . as if I had an unlimited supply of the stuff. I was unaware of the truth of my reality. Then, in one dark and life-changing moment, in the middle of the night, the earth stood still!

It was exactly 3:30 a.m. when I found myself sitting straight up in bed, literally screaming in pain! I was at my wits' end. Regardless of what I did, I could not escape the piercing, stabbing agony. My neck and shoulder felt as though a million needles had suddenly been thrust into me. My husband did his best to comfort me, but to no avail. The sheer pain was unbearable! We decided to head for the hospital. After hours of tormenting pain in the emergency room and enough brain-numbing medication to stop an elephant, not to mention numerous x-rays, I was finally sent home without a diagnosis.

The following few days were a blur, but after several visits to my doctor, an MRI revealed that the cause was an old whiplash injury precipitated by a head-on automobile accident that occurred when I was a teen and exacerbated when I was thrown from a horse some years later.

Days turned into weeks, weeks became months, and months eventually turned into two and half years before I started to lead some semblance of a normal life again. During that period, I had plenty of time to contemplate that face in the bathroom mirror again. Isn't it interesting how life makes decisions for you when you neglect to make them for yourself?

Then and there, I decided I was tired of unconsciously letting life live me. It was time for me to stop doing and start being. Each morning, as I contemplated my reflection in the mirror, I began to reminisce, allowing my mind to take me all the way back to my childhood. This mental journey helped me to recall how effortless it was to make decisions during those early years. Then suddenly—like a blast from the past—I remembered: "Lemonade, pickles and worms!"

CHAPTER ONE

ANOTHER TIME

*Cherish your visions and your dreams as they are the children of your
soul; the blueprints of your ultimate achievements.*

~ Napoleon Hill

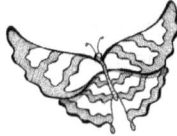

Once upon a time

It was a time long forgotten—but not completely lost. The
memories at first returned in intermittent flashes of vague,
unrelated thoughts and ideas, then morphed into clear and
complete visions long ago tucked away in the back of my mind—a
time when life seemed simpler and less complicated—a time
when I knew *who* I was, *what* I wanted and *where* I wanted to go. I
was totally unconcerned with the *how*, I just knew! At seven years
of age, I just knew and couldn't explain *why*, nor did I care to.

I'm the youngest of three children from an average middle
class family. As the youngest, I had the run of the house and my
needs were generally met, but like most children, I always wanted
more.

My father had a good job and made a sustainable income, and
my mother was a stay-at-home mom. But they had grown up in
and lived through the great depression and a world war.
Although more than twenty years had passed since the end of the
war, much of the pain of that era lingered in the memories of an
entire generation. Not surprisingly, comments like "Money

doesn't grow on trees" and "A penny saved is a penny earned" and "We are not the snooty rich folks on the west side of town" were common fare at our supper table.

Now, I was a firm believer in the "penny saved" concept, and I still am, but at that time my twenty-five-cent allowance didn't last long enough to get past the local ice cream vendor, let alone make it to the bank. It didn't take me long to understand that my parents were committed to taking care of most everything I *needed*, but if I *wanted* something, I would have to find another resource. This was the "Aha!" moment that really started my wheels turning.

Although I didn't consciously sit down and analyze my financial state of affairs, somewhere deep inside me, my intuition suggested that this stuff called money had something to do with getting the things I wanted. I also hypothesized (in a very rudimentary way) that if I wasn't getting enough of something *I wanted*, then I had to give more of what *somebody else wanted* in return.

Out of the mouths of babes! It doesn't get much simpler than that, does it?

At age seven I really couldn't explain the concept, yet I knew intuitively what to do. It certainly wasn't that I was a genius or a child prodigy; it was just that there wasn't anyone to tell me I couldn't think what I wanted or that I couldn't do whatever I decided.

Fortunately, my age and small size rendered me insignificant enough so that no one bothered to tell me that I was too young, too old, too short, too tall, too cute, too ugly, too dumb, too smart, or too anything. So as far as I was concerned, whatever I could believe and conceive, I could achieve. I just didn't yet know all I needed to know, since I hadn't had the benefit of all the great advice society had yet to bestow upon me!

An entrepreneur is born

Now, you have to understand that I didn't have a clue as to the *how, where* or *when*, I just knew the *what*, which was to put money in my pocket. The big emotional *why* translated into the things I wanted—ice cream cones, chili dogs, a new hat to wear, a book to read, another stuffed animal to add to my dog collection, and a very pronounced feeling of pride and independence.

One day, as I was serving lemonade to my various dolls and stuffed animals, a light bulb suddenly switched on in my imaginatively active young brain. Since I was already making and serving lemonade, instead of drinking up what I reasoned could be potential profits, maybe what I should be doing would be to invite real people with real money. Hence, the birth of my first lemonade stand. Business was a little slow at first, but since my mother donated all the ingredients, every cup sold was pure profit.

It wasn't long before those dimes and nickels turned into real folding money. By then I was hooked. It was a great feeling not having to ask for an ice cream cone when I was out with my family. And if I saw a hat I liked while shopping with my mother, I just reached in my purse and bought it. Unfortunately, the lemonade business was seasonal at best and subject to sudden temperature and weather changes. I needed a more consistent cash flow, and at my age that meant money in my purse that I could not only count, but count on, as well.

Diversification (pickles, of course!)

Have you ever noticed that when you're clear about something you want, you start seeing that thing—or manifestations of a similar idea—everywhere you look?

Some call it the Law of Attraction, others say it's a coincidence or maybe just dumb luck. I can only say that through the years, I have personally found that whenever I put my attention on my intention, the *who, where* and *how* details magically reveal themselves.

My introduction to the pickle business was no exception.

Not far from where we lived there was a cucumber processing plant, better known as a pickle factory. At the end of each day they would throw out the cucumbers that didn't meet their specifications. There was nothing wrong with them; they were just too long, too fat, or too something. I decided the little red wagon in which I used to pull my stuffed animals around the neighborhood would be perfect for hauling pickles. The rest is history. I found out that I could show up at the factory at closing time and they would give me all the "reject" pickles my wagon could hold. So, when it was too cold to sell lemonade, I started going door-to-door, pulling my wagon behind me. And guess what? People actually bought my rejected pickles. I became the neighborhood pickle girl. When I wasn't selling lemonade, I was peddling pickles. Life was good—until one day it started raining.

M S I: (multiple sources of income)

Every time it rained, my purse became lighter and lighter. The rainy season had arrived, and my hard-won booty was rapidly dissipating. Now, since I wasn't an adult yet and didn't know I was supposed to be disappointed, frustrated, worried, and over-whelmed with fear and ambivalence, I stayed calm and relatively happy, and I continued to keep my attention on my intention.

I kept my focus on the "what" and turned up the volume of my emotional "why," and, lo and behold, I was soon rewarded with another "how."

The neck of the woods I grew up in just happened to be very popular with outdoorsmen, and fishing was one of the number one pastimes. As a matter of fact, if you didn't fish, some folks might consider you a beer or two short of a six-pack.

Well, my grandfather owned a business that provided stock for the local bait shops. He would go out on damp, rainy nights and harvest live fishing worms from the soggy soil—not your garden-variety fishing worm, mind you, but a somewhat oversized, slimy creature affectionately known to local anglers as a "night crawler." These much-sought-after creatures of the earth could most easily be harvested at night—and preferably during a good rain.

A good rain? Was this a miraculous confluence of divine intervention or just a coincidence? I didn't waste one extra second considering the merits of such philosophical questions. All I knew for sure was that I had found a way to fill the gaping void in my ailing income stream.

I ended up working beside my dad and grandfather, pulling night crawlers out of the wet ground at the going rate of two cents a pop. My grandfather considered me an independent contractor, and I was able to keep everything I earned. It wasn't long before I was back in the money again.

Lonely at the top

Between the ages of seven and twelve, in addition to lemonade, pickles and worms, I chalked up a total of eleven income opportunities. Whenever I downloaded an idea from what some people call "that thinking stuff," I would just get excited about the "why," and the "how" would always manifest itself in some way—no exceptions.

As I started flourishing financially, though, I noticed an interesting phenomenon. Some of my girlfriends, whom I thought of as close, slowly became distant. A few even became quite vocal about it, suggesting that I thought I was special or that I had in some way violated a cardinal rule of girlhood friendship. My insecurities began to mount. I found myself personally embarrassed, carefully hiding from almost everyone the fact that I traded worms for money.

It was true that I enjoyed nice things and always tried to maintain a color-coordinated wardrobe, a trait I inherited from my mother. But I have to say, I didn't really do it for her or my girlfriends. In fact, I naïvely thought they would be excited for me. Mom was, of course, but reality finally set in when I discovered the insidious nature of jealousy among young girls. I tried to explain to them that I had extra money in my purse because I worked for it and earned it. It soon became obvious that my critical friends preferred to believe that I was just another over-indulged child who had somehow changed. Others went as far as to suggest that every new idea I came up with was foolhardy, a waste of time, and couldn't possibly be accomplished by anyone, let alone an insignificant little girl like me.

Although I was still only a child, I was being introduced to the adult concept of dream stealing. Later in life, although I had successfully grown into adulthood as a self-directed, determined young woman, I came to know that much of my experience while growing up had shaped my ability to manifest my life's destiny and that identifying and understanding past belief systems had been an invaluable asset.

Though some may be tempted to dismiss the precepts that guided me when I was young as so much child's play, I am firmly convinced that early influences and experiences, good or bad, do indeed get packed away in the subconscious mind. These hidden emotions will ultimately influence and affect many of the most important decisions we make throughout our individual lives.

* * * * *

If you carry your childhood with you, you never become older.

~ Tom Stoppard

Chapter One Summary

Another Time

- Get in touch with and invite your inner child back into your life.
- Your divine essence is still there waiting for you.
- If you begin to neutralize old disempowering beliefs, you can then develop new perceptions about your life that serve you.
- As long as you know with clarity, "what" you want and attach a big enough emotional "why," the "how" will reveal itself.
- Childhood interests and experiences, good or bad, have bigger impacts on our lives as adults than we realize.

Self Coaching Questions. Your answers are only as good as the questions you ask! Here are some suggestions. Use a separate piece of paper to answer each question to determine if your perceptions and beliefs of the past still serve you today.

Think Back . . .

- List the limiting beliefs you may have adopted as a child that you feel have had an effect on your decision making today.
- Are there any patterns of behavior that you can see?
- What did you enjoy as a child? What did you daydream about?
- What personal gifts can you identify that set you apart from other people? List them.
- How could you apply those gifts today?
- Do you let other people and circumstances steal your dreams? Who are they to you? Why do you think they do this? And more importantly, ask yourself, why do you allow this?

CHAPTER TWO

ROSE-COLORED GLASSES

What we see depends mainly on what we look for.

~ John Lubbock

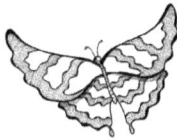

Through a child's eyes

Let's face it, we look at life differently when we're kids. Back then, everything we saw, heard, smelled, tasted or touched was new, fresh, exciting, and contained the promise of infinite possibility. Our life then was teeming with wonder, adventure, and an intuitive sense of being alive.

Nothing mattered except what was going on right here and right now! We had no concept of the past or the future, and the word "ego" hadn't yet entered our vocabulary. To us, yesterday was already a dream and tomorrow was just a vision. Somehow, even absent the ability to articulate the idea, we knew that just by appreciating today we could make every yesterday a dream of happiness and every tomorrow a vision of infinite possibility.

So what happened to that idyllic state of being? Why does life today often seem so stressful, so mundane, and so dull?

As adults, we pride ourselves on our "knowledge" of the spiritual concepts of ancient sages, yet we sometimes fail miserably at the simple task of feeling good. Suffering seems to be the norm, and a moment of bliss is rare and fleeting. Happiness seems to have been degraded until the word no longer has any meaning. It's as if some insidious disease has infected the very fabric of our soul!

Green or brown?

When I was a child, my consciousness was dominated by a wonderful palette of beautiful hues of green: satisfaction, courage, assurance, certainty, joy, happiness, confidence, love and abundance. At some point, though, I started being told, "Stop looking at the world through rose-colored glasses and start taking notice of realities."

As I grew from childhood into young adulthood, I began to notice a different "color" gradually permeating my emotional environment. It really wasn't a *new* color; my sense memory told me that it had been there all the time. I just had not been looking for it because I was too busy with optimism and productive activity. It wasn't until other people pointed it out that I finally began noticing that this new "color" (the brown of life) came in various shades of disappointment, fear, worry, doubt, envy, despair, inferiority feelings, and an increasing sense of lack.

Over time, I was convincingly persuaded that everything wasn't "peaches and cream." I needed to become a responsible adult, they told me, and I needed to be more realistic and stop dreaming so much!

As I grew up, my parents, friends, and associates—even some of my teachers—continued to school me on the merits of "responsibility." I began to notice that my personal results often supported the apparent validity of their wisdom.

Things didn't always seem to work out anymore. Even worse, I had to be careful so I wouldn't be taken advantage of. People didn't seem to be as honest any longer. Money was harder to come by and didn't seem to buy as much. The market was up, the market was down; the economy was good, the economy was bad. I also noticed that it was raining more than it used to; sunny days seemed few and far between. There was always too much month left at the end of the money. There were credit cards to pay off, the mortgage, car repairs, utilities, doctor bills and — oh, yes — let's not forget the out-of-sight prices of fuel, both for the car and the body. And what about hurricanes, tornadoes, fires, earthquakes, floods and the world trade center? Yup, they were right. I'd better keep every waking thought focused on this stuff or the world will surely go to hell in a hand basket. One last thing: I don't know what it was, but I didn't seem to be feeling as good as I used to, either.

The question is: What do you see more of when you go to the party of life — "green" or "brown?" Whichever it is for you, is that a perception or a reality? I have personally seen both at the same party, good and bad. So we ask the question: "Is this a good party or a bad one?"

There's a widely held concept that our ability to enjoy any party (including life itself) will depend heavily on what we each go to that party to see, feel, think, or discover. In other words, your opinion of that party — and of life itself in any given moment — will be constantly determined and re-determined by your personal perception and intention.

The point is that when I was a child, I didn't know I couldn't do wonderful and productive things, yet I proved I could because I did. How was I able to do those things with relatively little effort as a youngster, yet had a much harder time coping later on? Was it just the disparity between childhood circumstances and the reality of adult issues, or is it something much deeper?

After all, here I am, staring at the face of transition in my bathroom mirror, trying to get out of my own way. I invite you to consider the possibility that maybe (just maybe) we are all so used to looking at the "brown" of life that we have a hard time recognizing the beautiful "green" that has always been there.

Maybe those old rose-colored glasses revealed more truth than most of us would care to admit!

* * * * *

If we could see the miracle of a single flower clearly,
our whole life would change.

~ Buddha

Chapter Two Summary

Rose-Colored Glasses

- See every day with the eyes of new possibilities.
- Look for the green; remember, if you change the way you look at things in your life, those things in your life you're looking at will change.

Self Coaching Questions. Your answers are only as good as the questions you ask! Here are some suggestions. Use a separate piece of paper to answer each question to determine if your perceptions and beliefs of the past still serve you today.

What Do You See?

- Take inventory of your thoughts. Are you looking for what you want or what you don't want in life?
- What do you see in your life today that is wonderful?
- Which do you see when you look at the word "Nowhere?"
    - "Opportunity is *No where*" or
    - "Opportunity is *Now here?*"

CHILD'S PLAY - STORY #1

UNPACKAGED HOPES, EMPTY DREAMS

Empty boxes

"Wake up! Today, we are going downtown to do some shopping," says my mother, her head and shoulders sticking out from behind the partially opened door of my room. I jump out of bed, hurry to wash up and get dressed, and eat a quick breakfast on the run. An exciting day ahead, indeed!

Before pulling the car out of the garage, mom checks the gas gauge to make sure we have enough fuel to make the drive, and she also snaps open her wallet to see whether there is enough cash there for what looks like might be a major shopping spree.

The drive always seems endless but the downtown shopping district is only 20 minutes away. On the way, I gaze out of the car window and admire the large, historic homes on streets lined with huge, old oak trees on both sides. Spring is in the air today, and the smells of the various flowers blooming are so sweet that their fragrances almost give me a sugar taste in my mouth.

We locate a parking spot near the blocks where the stores are, and the adventure begins. Our first stop is Jacobson's, a beautifully appointed department store. Mom loves to browse through the various departments, while I make my way like an arrow in flight to the children's clothing section, where I immediately spot four beautiful outfits that would look perfect on me. I gather them up and place each item carefully on the counter outside the fitting rooms, but I'm only six, so the sales ladies won't let me take clothes to the dressing room until my mother is there to supervise. So I wait—and wait—and finally, here comes Mom, and off we go into the magic, mirror-filled rooms. One by one, I try on the outfits I've picked out. When I have each one looking just right, I walk out to the mirrors on the sales floor and the sales ladies "Ooh" and "Ahh" about how pretty I look in each and every outfit—Mom agrees with them every time. Of course, I want them all, but Mom reminds me that "we're not made of money" and "there'll be plenty of new clothes for you when the new school year starts—and you might be much bigger then." Inside myself, I'm thinking that I'd be happy to take just one outfit home with me right now. But after all that, we leave Jacobson's with no packages in hand.

We wander slowly down the street, peering into the display windows of each new store and admiring what we see—the displays are filled with brightly colored summer items. Soon we come to Winkleman's, a woman's store that my mother really admires. Nothing there for me, but the sales clerks are always helpful and pleasant and call my mother by name, even when she doesn't buy anything, which turns out to be the case today. We also stop in The Hat Box, which is filled with hundreds of hats in every color, shape and size. But despite the big selection, Mom can't make a decision, and we leave there, too, empty-handed.

We walk by store after store but buy nothing. All of a sudden it's noon and I've worked up an appetite. Worse, I can smell something terrific and wonderful—the smell is coming from across the street—from S. S. Kresge's (Mom calls it a five-and-dime store), but all I know is that they serve the very best chili dogs ever.

Before I can even ask to stop to eat, Mom reminds me that we'll be eating lunch at home and we need to leave very soon. So we cross the street, reverse direction, and head back toward our car, but Mom decides to make one more stop along the way. We visit a store I've never been in before, a specialty leather store. The moment we open the door, we're enveloped in the rich, dark look and feel of expensive leather and by a smell so wonderful that it almost knocks me off my feet. Mom looks at purses, wallets, gloves, even leather coats, and I can tell she's impressed and tempted, but I am sure she doesn't see anything of interest, since we leave the store without buying anything. So, after about three hours of looking but not buying, away we go, headed back home!

What a day! I had a wonderful time, but the thought of those outfits that I spent so much time looking at and trying on and then not buying even one of them leaves me wondering why we spent all that time and returned home with no boxes. I thought we were going shopping! I know my mother loves me, so why can't I add some new clothes to my closet?

Once home, Mom seems unusually quiet as she makes our soup and sandwiches. It seems like she has other things on her mind. It reminds me of me when I'm daydreaming. For just a moment I wonder if moms daydream, too, but a few minutes later the moment (and my thought) has passed, and I'm enjoying a cucumber sandwich—my favorite sandwich of all. But I can't help thinking about the clothes that I wanted. Why do I always have to be so patient?

CHAPTER THREE

CORPORATE CRAP

*Life is a mirror and will reflect back to the thinker
what he thinks into it.*

~ Ernest Holmes

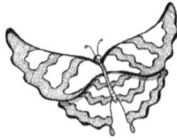

Is that all there is?

How time flies for all of us! We survived the emotional maze of early childhood, navigated our way through grammar school, battled through puberty and somehow, through it all, managed to acquire a formal education.

It all happened so fast that we couldn't help but wonder if we had touched all the bases, but it was too late to think about that. We were suddenly responsible adults, and (ready or not) society was telling us that it was time to get off the old rusty-dusty, head out into the world, and earn a living.

So that's what we did. We each put on our professional face, painstakingly wrote a concise, comprehensive résumé, donned our best "I mean business" attire, hit the pavement, and—depending on our education level and personal preferences—landed our first job, opened our first office, or started our first business.

Since this isn't a "how to find a job or start your own business" book, I'm not going to spend a lot of time discussing the pros and cons of each, except to point out two things:

1. First, whether we are serving a single boss, a handful of clients, or a whole database full of customers, we all need to learn the professional attributes of becoming a first-rate sales person since we will eventually realize, if we haven't already, that we will spend the rest of our life selling ourselves.

2. And second, the word security has no meaning regardless of what career path we choose. Security and joy are perceptions we must develop within ourselves and take with us.

Unfortunately, most of us were not given either the time or the opportunity while we were young to explore ourselves thoroughly to find out who we really are and to discover the inner joy we are all capable of.

In fact, we were told to believe that happiness was something we'd find "out there," and once having found it, we could finally be "happy." But over and over again, as we gradually achieved or acquired something we thought we wanted, we discovered that the joy of victory was short-lived, at best. We no sooner reached one coveted goal than we found ourselves immediately searching for another, always looking for more, always striving for something better, always believing that once we reached that next goal, then at last we could truly be happy.

All the world loves a winner!

My parents taught me to always do my best at anything I was doing. This penchant for perfection became a habit and spilled over into my working environment. Since I loved ice cream, I guess it was no surprise that I secured my first "real" job working in an ice cream parlor. At age 13, with a special work permit in hand, I was on the payroll. I appreciated the accolades I received from the owner, and I had fun serving the customers, as well as enjoying the added benefit of having access to all the ice cream I could eat!

I decided making money and having fun were two key ingredients for a successful career. The advantage of this strategy was, the more jobs I engaged in, the closer I came to identifying my interests, abilities, natural talents and passions. The ice cream parlor was the first in a long line of job opportunities.

Curiously, during all of the J.O.B. activity, my childhood entrepreneurial spirit had taken a back seat to the so-called "security" of a regular paycheck. I allowed myself to become mesmerized by what I perceived at the time as "moving up the ladder." I eventually became a bona fide member of the proverbial rat race and unconsciously began trading the days of my life for someone else's dream!

But still, there I was! I had finally arrived — or so I thought. After I had taken advantage of a series of career-building opportunities in sales and marketing, I invested my heart and soul in the real estate industry. I landed a position with a major home builder/developer in a new and rapidly growing city where my husband and I had decided to live. I accepted a position as an on-site residential sales representative and community manager.

The company was the largest real estate operation in the region, and I loved my job. Understanding that the purchase of a home is the single largest investment most people will make in their life, I enjoyed serving the home buyers I worked with, and I got along very well with the people I worked for.

The company didn't offer the same compensation and benefits package for sales people as for executive management, but the commission-based pay plan was very generous, and I liked the idea of writing my own ticket. I had the support and respect of the executive management team and the cooperation and admiration of my peers. I felt happy, empowered, and productive. All in all, I had a very healthy sense of confidence and well-being.

Then something terrible happened! I became very successful!

What's so terrible about that? Nothing, if you define success as being the top producer with the highest conversion ratio in the entire company; nothing, if you enjoy financial abundance; and nothing, as long as you actually enjoy the process. So again, what's the problem?

As my sales portfolio grew, so did my confidence. Although I understood that true confidence is knowing that you know, I also understood that arrogance was pretending you know. Because I was very careful to recognize the difference, my ability to maintain the cooperation and admiration of my peers seemed to be a testament to my effectiveness in the field.

Although management would occasionally elicit feedback from their troops in the field, it was clear their inquiries had less to do with formulating new strategies and more to do with garnering support for decisions already made behind closed doors. Believing my input might actually be well received, I responded to their inquiries by making suggestions and raising issues I thought might be in everyone's best interest. However, I found management's response to my input somewhat cold. My sixth sense informed me something was amiss, but I just couldn't put my finger on it.

"So . . . you must think you're pretty special!"

It wasn't until I was sitting in the vice president's office on a sunny Tuesday morning, waiting for what I thought was going to be an "attaboy" for my stellar performance and suggestions, that I was finally shocked into the realization of how naïve I had been. Without so much as a "Good morning," the boss' first words were, "So . . . you must think you're pretty special!"

The combination of his words and his tone of voice instantly whisked me back to the stinging memory of having to justify my success to those misinformed, misguided and very jealous, self-centered seven-year-old girlfriends.

As the boss droned on, criticizing and finger-pointing, my brain whirled. I couldn't understand why this was happening. Then, suddenly, I got it! I was making too much money! Since I was on commission and making lots of sales, I was actually making more money than many of the salaried executive management staff!

So, there I was again, standing alone with my empty pickle wagon and a purse full of money, trying to make some sense out of nonsense. Alas! Some things never change!

Reaction vs. Response

At that moment, though, I hadn't focused on my lemonade, pickles and worms experiences. I was an adult now, and that was just so much "kid stuff." In this situation, it was time to make some adult decisions.

At first I was at a total loss. After the VP decided he had succeeded in "setting me straight," he suggested that I might want to watch my step in the future. I left his office in "shock and awe" — frustrated, disappointed and dejected.

As the next several weeks dragged on, I found myself working harder and enjoying it less. Buyers seemed less co-operative, and getting anything through corporate was a challenge at best. I still maintained my status as a top producer, but I was no longer honored as a shining example. I noticed, too, that not only did the executive management staff make life miserable, but other people I worked with — folks I was sure were well beyond the drama — seemed to turn a cold shoulder at times. I felt bullied, manipulated and very disconnected.

I finally realized that not only was I not having fun any more, but also I no longer felt good about myself. I often found myself in a repetitive, knee-jerk, reactive mode. Every time somebody would throw a ball in my direction, I felt compelled to catch it and then figure out the best way to throw it back. The emotional, mental and physical energy it took to justify and defend my every move became overwhelming and was damaging every aspect of my life. I was tired of playing the corporate game, and it was obviously time to move on.

I knew my decision was an appropriate response, but I was still unable to ignore the drama. Although I found a new position with a competitor in the same city and soon became their number one producer, I would occasionally run into people I knew from the old company. Whenever this would occur, I would irrationally reason that I was still being criticized and talked about. My emotions took over! As a result, I became very self-conscious, reverted back to reactionary thinking, and decided that the only reasonable thing to do was to move out of the area completely.

Believing this was what I needed to do, I sold the house, packed up our belongings, and got out of town leaving behind enormous income potential by turning my back on one of the hottest real estate markets in the country.

Cause and Effect

In hindsight, I can see that I was reacting to an old, disempowering event—an event that sparked the memory of a negatively charged emotion that I had long since tucked away and forgotten in my subconscious mind. I believed I was responding to the cause of my suffering, but I was actually reacting to an effect. While I thought I was responding appropriately to the vice president's criticism, I was really still dealing with the old, misinformed childhood judgments of my peers.

It's clear to me now that when we lose sight of the significance of the causes of past pain, we react to every current effect as if it were a primary cause, and we continue to experience a lifetime of unintentional, unwarranted, and unnecessary confusion, ambivalence and suffering.

Many of the great sages in history and in our time have suggested that looking back and understanding the past can be the window through which we can truly see our future. It has also been said that the ability to forgive ourselves and others is the only way to prevent the sometimes irreversible damage that guilt, resentment and blame can have on the human condition.

Again, maybe we should all take the time to contemplate that familiar face in the bathroom mirror—not just the image that reflects itself back, but the powerful spirit and true "You" that resides behind those searching eyes.

Oh, by the way, I *am* special—and so are *you*!

* * * * *

The weak can never forgive.
Forgiveness is the attribute of the strong.

~ Mahatma Gandhi

Chapter Three Summary

Corporate Crap

- Past events are sometimes tucked away and forgotten in the subconscious mind only to cause inappropriate reactions to present circumstances.
- Drama filled current circumstances are more likely an effect of negative emotions caused by past events long forgotten.
- Look back to your beginnings and rediscover your true spirit!

Self Coaching Questions. Your answers are only as good as the questions you ask! Here are some suggestions. Use a separate piece of paper to answer each question to determine if your perceptions and beliefs of the past still serve you today.

What Pushes Your Buttons?

- What kinds of experiences trigger your negative emotions today? List them.
- How can you relate your reactions to present experiences to events from the past?
- What common thread seems to connect your reaction to the past in relationship to your response to present events?

CHAPTER FOUR

TICK TOCK

*The past is gone. The future isn't here yet,
nor is it guaranteed. Every day is a gift.
That's why they call it the present!*

~ Author Unknown

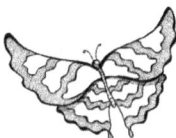

In the blink of an eye

I'm short of time! There's not enough time! This is taking too much time! This is a waste of time! I haven't got time for that! The days feel as though they're getting progressively shorter and there just aren't enough hours in a day. Everything we do, say or feel seems to be confined by this unobtainable entity called "time," yet we revere its imagined existence—as if we had some control over it. We can't feel, touch, smell, hear or even see it, but our whole life seems to revolve around (and depend upon) that elusive task master, we call time. We wake up at its beck and call, we eat by it, sleep by it, and literally live by its rule. Yet we can never seem to find enough of it. Then, one day, in a blink of an eye, we are told, "Time's up," and we find ourselves wondering where it all went!

Are we there yet?

If we think back to childhood, we will probably realize that today we think of time quite differently than we did then. How many of us can remember those good old school days that seemed never to end? It wasn't that we didn't appreciate the opportunity for an education, it's just that we had more important things on our minds. There were trees that needed climbing, softball games that needed playing, and just the business of being a kid that needed to be taken care of. I had come to the conclusion that all the clocks on school property must have inherited the same mechanical dysfunction, since none of them appeared to work. School days often seemed to drag on so long that by the time the bell rang, you would swear you must have fallen asleep and awakened the next day. Car trips with the family were even worse; the resounding "Are we there yet?" was a familiar cry. My idea of tomorrow was "sometime in the future." Next week was too far away even to think about, and next month just didn't exist. So why the disparity? Haven't we always had 24 hours a day to work with? Maybe it has to do with how we used to define time!

What time is it—really?

The concept of time appears to be relatively simple, but its ramifications can (and do) have critical—and sometimes potentially disastrous—effects on our ability to live a healthy, joyful and stress-free life. In fact, psychologists and other experts tell us that the way in which we perceive time can and will make the difference as to whether we succeed in using it to enhance our lives as opposed to allowing it to use us. Things sure were simpler when the only thing that mattered was now!

* * * * *

My pre-school days were relatively uneventful, as far as I can recall. I do remember being totally preoccupied with the new and wondrous adventures before me. I had very little "past" to contemplate and I scarcely had the insight to conceptualize what a future meant, let alone to consider what that might look like. Free of such distractions from the past or future, I was completely conscious, with my present awareness focused only on the right here and right now. And what a glorious state that was! I didn't have time to be mad, sad or disappointed; and if I did, it never lasted long. My focus was on the joy, and there was no way I was going to miss out on that!

This was probably the only time I can remember when I was purely, naturally and completely with myself, fully experiencing the magnificent gift of life. With no defined future to be anxious or worried about and no past to feel guilty about, I just didn't have enough history to manifest resentment, guilt or blame. If anything created a concern, it was short lived, and it quickly dissipated in the flood of joy, excitement, and power I felt in my unfolding new life. As I look back, I wonder what my life today would be like if I had been able to maintain that glorious state of conscious awareness throughout my school years and adult history.

"Clock time" vs. "Real time"

Some people may feel compelled to react to the last paragraph by suggesting that being "in the now" and having fun as an infant or toddler is all well and good, but that adults have more serious responsibilities and their lives are infinitely more complicated. In addition, people may also question that although the concept of time can often be a pain, it is also a very necessary evil. Based on the popular definition of time that most people believe to be true, they would be right.

But what if there is another idea of "time" that transcends the mental concept of *clock time*? And what if *real time* is "a real experience" as opposed to the illusion of *clock time*?

Let's look a little deeper into this idea and explore what it really means. The confusion comes when we insist there is only one kind of time and one definition. To most of us, we relate everything that happens in our life as "clock time." This is obviously a very necessary tool we all use to navigate our life. Everything we think about, plan for, and do on a physical plane relies on our ability to efficiently and effectively coordinate life around the clock and calendar. One of the reasons we continue to experience stress, ambivalence, and suffering may be because clock and calendar time never stand still.

Imagine this: how much stress and suffering would we avoid if we could manipulate time; for example, if we could make time stand still at will?

Before we could allow ourselves to accept such an illogical idea, we would need to accept the concept that suggests we can only live our lives now — not yesterday, not tomorrow — but today, in the "now!" Since the human mind is only capable of thinking one action, one feeling, and one thought at a time, if all our thoughts are focused on past or fixated on future time, there's no time for "real time," which is right now today! Consequently, since life can only be lived in the present, we end up missing most of our life. If everything we do or think is about yesterday, or everything we do or think is a means to an end for tomorrow, it follows there will be no today to live.

I feel the answer to this dilemma, as Eckhart Tolle explains in his book, *A New Earth*, is to find a way to appreciate the now, and the only way to do that is to recognize the existence of another definition for time: a separate understanding of time that transcends the clock and calendar. A realization, if you will, that now is the only real time, and without it we are simply letting our life pass us by.

Think back as far as you can, maybe even before the demands of going to school and trying to grow up. Remember when the only time was the present and the only thing that really mattered was whatever you were doing at that very moment. Your only objective was to enjoy that moment, and any unplanned obstacle was only temporary, since your focus and intent was to appreciate, embrace and experience all the wonders and adventure life had to offer. You didn't regret the past, and you welcomed the future as it unfolded. Unencumbered by the past or the future, every day was a new day, and every new day was a day to be savored. We rarely had to wait for the end of the week to exclaim, "Thank God it's Friday" because our attention was on our intention, and that intention was to have fun and feel good.

Unfortunate, isn't it, that as we grow up and get "smart," we usually lose in some way or other that divine ability to dream, imagine, create and be consciously present without trying.

Of course, some present moments aren't as comfortable and effortless as we would like. But if we truly care about how we *feel*, then we must have the deliberate intention to *feel good*. The challenge now, and perhaps the imperative, is to get that capability back. Maybe if we stop running from the pain, we can!

When we consciously accept and embrace any feeling that might appear uncomfortable to us, the uncomfortable feeling tends to transform itself into something positive quite gratuitously. By living our lives in *real time*, our future will be on track. The way we feel is an indicator of the direction we are heading and that is primarily determined by what and how we choose to think!

Bottom line, every evening will be Friday night, and every day will be the beginning of another weekend, as long as we decide to use our *clock time* only as it was intended—as a measuring stick, not as an imperative. Once we enthusiastically embrace our *real time*, we will have the best possible opportunity to experience each and every moment of our glorious life ***now!***

* * * * *

One day at a time – this is enough.
Do not look back and grieve over the past, for it is gone;
and do not be troubled about the future, for it has not yet come.
Live in the present, and make it so beautiful
that it will be worth remembering.

~ Ida Scott Taylor

Chapter Four Summary

Tick Tock

- Time is an illusion.
- Life only really exists right here, right now, at this moment in time.
- As long as your deliberate intention is to show up and live life now, time will become your personal servant rather than an all consuming master.
- Trying to live life in the past, or in the future, will only cause you to miss the present.

Self Coaching Questions. Your answers are only as good as the questions you ask! Here are some suggestions. Use a separate piece of paper to answer each question to determine if your perceptions and beliefs of the past still serve you today.

The Time is Now!

- Do you spend time thinking about yesterday, today or tomorrow?
- What activities seem to make your time fly by so quickly that you lose all sense of this thing called "time?"
- Could this be a clue of what activities you resonate with?
- What activities would you participate in if time wasn't a factor?

GAMES WON,
MOMENTS LOST

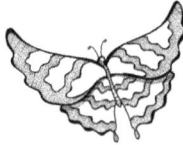

Blooper ball and caramel apples

"It's blooper ball season again!" my dad yells. "Get ready; we are going to the Hoyt Park Ball Field tonight for my first game of the season. We will be leaving no later than 5:15 p.m. so I can warm up for the game."

Dad is the pitcher for the team. During the week, when he comes home from work, I spend hours preparing him for the game, acting as catcher for his practice and warm-ups. I received my very own ball glove when I was four years old and I now proudly hang it in my closet. (Sometimes I think my dad wanted another son!)

With all the excitement, we arrive at the ball park and locate the ball diamond that Sam's Tavern, my dad's team, will be playing on. It doesn't take long to spot the team since the team wears bright royal blue and gold team shirts. We are certainly not early; colorful blankets are already spread all across the green grass from one end of the park to the other. We locate our favorite spot, throw the blanket down along with a cooler that is filled with beverages and snacks, and open a folding chair for my mother to relax in.

The game is soon underway! I notice that George's Traveling Snack Truck is here again this year. The truck is painted in bright colors and decorated with red candy apples, baby pink cotton candy and buttered popcorn. As soon as the truck pulls up, people immediately stop whatever they are doing at the time and head directly to the truck. The air is filled with the most delicious smells. The lines are long, but everyone is leaving with freshly popped popcorn, caramel apples that are dipped in nuts, hard red candy apples, caramel corn, candies of all sorts and a variety of cold drinks. My mouth simply drools when I see the families pass by with all the sweet goodies.

It's about now that my mother opens the cooler and passes out snacks from home. I couldn't help but ask "Could I have a caramel apple smothered with nuts?" It is suggested maybe at the next game. My mother says, "We have brought our own snacks, plus you have just eaten a big supper at home. An apple like that is a bit too big and heavy on the stomach anyway."

After cheering on my dad's team, the game is finally over. His team has won. I am so happy for him, and most of all I enjoy seeing that extra big smile on his face when I know he is pleased. We neatly pack up everything. I can't wait until next week's big game. Who knows? I might just have an opportunity to sink my teeth into that caramel apple that I've been dreaming about!

CHAPTER FIVE

I AM WHAT I AM

My goal in life is to be
the kind of person my dog thinks I am!

~ Toby and Eileen Green

It's only me!

Who are you, anyway? If you've asked yourself this question lately and your answer is: "I don't know!"—you may already be on the right track.

The truth is, if you think you know who you are, *you are probably identifying with everything but who you really are.*

The logic here is that if you admit you don't know who you are anymore, you may be closer to knowing than you think. It's the simple act of "thinking" and trying to verbally express your idea of "you" that gets in the way of knowing your true self.

There is a widely held premise that true knowing knows no language because knowing is not a thought process, although language is. Deep, heartfelt knowing is a feeling experience. Thinking, however, tends to dredge up opinions, prejudices, pre-existing beliefs, and judgments that are mental belief systems, not true inner experiences. Simply put, if you have to think about it, it must, of course, be put into words; and if you have to do that, you are identifying with something that is not who you really are, anyway.

Let's expand on the concept of "knowing" by revisiting our childhood days.

As newborn infants—and for quite some time after that—we didn't have any way to describe what we saw or what we did. We just *felt*. We were our entire universe. But somehow, even without language, we found a way to communicate with the world by crying, smiling or laughing. We knew we were having an effect on those we communicated with because they responded by taking care of our needs. In other words, we received results by communicating. All this without language or complicated thought process—we just knew.

When I was a toddler, I wasn't even sure what my name was, so I really didn't know what to identify with. I didn't know I was a baby, a child, a girl, a sister or anything else. I just knew I was. Eventually, I realized my actions had an effect on others, and I learned that when people said my name . . . they were talking to me.

But for the most part, I was able to celebrate every waking moment without becoming attached to anything. I watched white, billowy clouds float by in the sky. I listened to the birds singing in the trees. I built castles in my sandbox and had tea parties with my stuffed animals. I imagined and pretended for hours on end. Being who and where I wanted by playing "make believe," at any given moment, was my reality "now." Every day there were new and exciting elements introduced into my environment. But since I didn't feel the need to identify with those changes, I rarely experienced any self-inflicted pain or suffering.

This began to change once I acknowledged my name and started to identify with all the labels that were being attached to me. I had to be a dutiful daughter, a good student, a loyal girlfriend, and I was required to meet my sociological obligations as a member of my family. I was expected to react to family pressures and to people's expectations in a manner that was consistent with my newfound "identity." In a way, I was beginning to lose my freedom as well as my innocence!

I naturally started to experience discomfort and occasional anxiety when I began to believe that I had to perform in such a way that garnered other people's approval. It wasn't long before who I was became obscured by who I was "supposed to be." As my social responsibilities expanded, so did my labels.

Depending upon who you asked, I was an entrepreneur, a spoiled little rich girl, an ungrateful sister, a successful career woman, or (as I mentioned earlier) "somebody special."

Functionally, things got more complicated, too. I was a parent to my dogs, a top producer for the company I worked for, a wife to my husband, all while still trying to maintain my status as a dutiful daughter and a loving sister. The truth was that *I* wasn't any of those things, except maybe the being special part; the tragedy was that I believed I was all of them.

At the time, I didn't realize that all the things I had identified with were only roles I was playing in this epic movie called "my life." Those things were not me at all. They were just other people's representations of who I was. Meanwhile, the real me was hidden away in moth balls gathering dust.

It was time to get back in touch with the real me!

Your authentic self

What I didn't know at the time was that my pain and suffering were products of the anxiety created by the uncertainty I experienced due to my ever-changing and expanding roles.

A mother, for instance, may feel unbearable emotional pain when a child leaves the nest. This is because of mom's identification with being a mom. She actually believes that's who she is. On the other hand, if she understands she is playing a role—the role of "mother"— then, as her child grows into adulthood, she can easily evolve into the more appropriate role of being a mentor and adult confidant rather than feeling lost when her child leaves.

In another scenario, when divorce happens or a spouse dies suddenly, a wife may feel lost and disconnected as she suddenly finds herself single again. She has identified with being a wife and an intimate partner of another and so may find it difficult to adjust to her new role as a self-sufficient, confident woman who is the director of her own destiny. Once she realizes this role is only one of many parts she will play on the stage of life, and that none of these roles is who she really is, she can then understand that she is not only the lead actress and director of her own story, but the screenwriter as well!

When we identify with our profession, social status, bank balance, personal health, possessions, appearance or accomplishments, we are identifying with life's illusions—every single one of which is subject to change.

The truth remains that our authentic self never changes. When we are attached to a role, once that role ends, and it will, we then set ourselves up for a lifetime of anxiety because we believe we've outlived our usefulness. The premise is the "real you" never dies. The essential self—the true self—is always present in each of us to provide joy, a passion for life and peace of mind if we strive to stay in touch with it.

All this, of course, speaks to the concept of truth versus perception. Perceptions are developed from old paradigms of beliefs we mistakenly label as truth. If we remember that a belief is nothing more than a thought that we think over and over again, and if we also understand all thoughts are not necessarily true, then it follows that many of our perceptions may not be grounded in reality. They are just perceptions, not necessarily truths. Our thoughts of who we think we are then become nothing more than an identification of what we do, how we look, and how we relate to others. Everything we identify with on the physical plane is subject to change. Our truth, our authentic self, is the only thing that never changes.

But again we ask, who is that?

Certainty vs. Uncertainty

As a child, I was rarely uncertain about anything. Actually, I don't believe I was at all familiar with the concept. I was absolutely certain about everything. I didn't have all the answers as to how it would come about, but I was certain I would have a life of health, wealth, and joy. In my mind, the world was my oyster.

As I grew though, I was reminded and conditioned by all those well-intentioned people around me that I needed to alter my outlook on life and to beware of change. When I started to observe the world through their eyes, I began to notice that everything did, indeed, change. I personally didn't judge change as either good or bad, but I did notice that many people seemed to harbor a great deal of anxiety when faced with the unfamiliar. Too much change seemed to breed a good deal of uncertainty in their minds, and this would generate a great deal of pain and suffering in their lives.

Recalling the years with my family, people in my neighborhood seldom moved away. I remember my parents didn't feel comfortable with change and therefore viewed anything new or innovative with skepticism and fear. They tolerated my childhood enterprises, but I was constantly reminded that buckling down and getting a good secure job and working hard was the only path to financial security. My parents were a product of the times, and any idea that appeared remotely unfamiliar was considered provocative, risky or uncertain at best. Truth be told, every new idea I came up with was viewed as just another wild hair up my behind!

You can imagine my family's dismay—even skeptical disbelief—when one day I announced my decision to leave home and move to another state to try my hand at paddling my own canoe.

Without really analyzing the concept of who I was, I had come to the realization that I needed to be me. I intuitively reasoned that whoever I was would always be within me and that would never change!

This inner knowing created the anchor in my life that helped me wean myself from having to identify with people, places, things and preconceived ideas. Those things always changed, but I knew I could handle anything life had to throw at me as long as I was confident about who I really was.

Eventually it taught me the lesson that complete certainty isn't necessarily a good thing, and that there always is—and almost always should be—some element of uncertainty in order to establish a balance in life. In other words, true peace of mind can't be achieved without a healthy balance of certainty and uncertainty.

I can't be sure, since my parents have crossed over, but I believe the source of a good deal of my parents' disillusionment about life actually revolved around the pure boredom they experienced as they tried to escape uncertainty instead of identifying with the pure joy of being. I am sure my mom and dad would agree that I am still very much a work in progress, but they would be pleased to know that my life's journey has afforded me the opportunity to be reintroduced to myself.

If I had only one wish, it would be that my parents could have had the same opportunity; and that is my wish for you, as well!

* * * * *

Happiness cannot be traveled to, owned,
earned, worn or consumed.
Happiness is the spiritual experience
of living every minute
with love, grace and gratitude.

~ Denis Waitley

Chapter Five Summary

I Am What I Am

- Knowing who you are is a heartfelt perception as opposed to a mental concept.
- Much of our suffering in life can be eliminated once we understand we are not our body or vocation, nor are we brothers, daughters, mothers, fathers, things or ideas; who you are is an all knowing experience that cannot be defined or explained.
- Playing roles, identifying with labels and mental ideas may change, but the "real you" always remains.
- Embrace the true you; strive only to be an effective steward to everything else and happiness and peace of mind will be your constant companions.
- The essence of you is that which never changes; this is your authentic self.
- Peace of mind means experiencing a healthy balance of certainty and uncertainty.

Self Coaching Questions. Your answers are only as good as the questions you ask! Here are some suggestions. Use a separate piece of paper to answer each question to determine if your perceptions and beliefs of the past still serve you today.

Who, Me?

- What are your beliefs and perceptions about yourself?
- Ask yourself, "Who is that, really, in the mirror?"
- What role do you identify most with?
- What kinds of feelings do you experience when you are "in the flow" and everything seems to fall into place?

CHAPTER SIX

YOU DON'T KNOW WHAT YOU DON'T KNOW

We must be willing to get rid of the life we've planned so as to have the life that is waiting for us!

~ Joseph Campbell

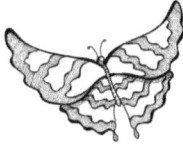

If only!

You've heard the old saying, "Hindsight is always 20/20." Many people would say that truer words were never spoken, and I once was one of them. It wasn't until later in my life that I realized interpretations made in the present about past decisions always appear very clear to us, yet in most cases they are misleading at best.

I'm sure you'll agree that yesterday's events can only be a memory, and any attempt to change any one of those events would be an absolute exercise in futility. You can never change what has already happened, but you can choose to think about the past in whatever way suits your needs best at any given time. The problem is, when needs change, so do memories. In other words, our memories of the past, regardless of their accuracy, are often altered to meet the needs of the present.

Of course, the only thing that really matters in this moment is what you do right here and right now. So why is it that people continually try to relive the past in the present by wishing they had done things differently then?

"If only I had done this" or "If only I hadn't done that." "If only I had taken more time to think" or "If only I had planned better then, things would be different now."

If only! If only!

Would've! Could've! Should've!

I'm embarrassed to say that until recently I suffered from this common affliction for a good portion of my adult life. Although I was pleased with many of my life's decisions, I always wondered how things might have been had I made different choices.

Shangri-La!

I was nineteen when I left the nest and headed to Florida to find fame and fortune. I packed my little sports car with everything but the kitchen sink, said my good-byes, and embarked on my first major adventure. Filled with optimism and enthusiasm, I was convinced I could handle anything life had to throw at me. And as time passed, I found I wasn't too far wrong. There were bumps in the road and a few detours along my life's path, but I always seemed to come out on top. I navigated a series of various employment opportunities, made new friends, developed new interests, met my life's partner, and had very little trouble enjoying each and every day, yet there was something that always seemed to nag at my spirit.

Although my job had me pulling up stakes and moving around the state from time to time, I actually stayed in Florida almost as long as I had with my family back home, and for me that was too long. This, coupled with my penchant for travel, had triggered my wanderlust, and it was starting to get the best of me. I was again considering the color of the grass on the other side of the fence. So off I went again seeking greener pastures, my Shangri-La if you will.

Looking for utopia, in and of itself, is generally perceived as a natural evolution that motivates people to grow and expand, provided they are doing it for the right reasons. Although most of my reasons were legitimate, I had unconsciously left behind some unresolved issues that would come back to haunt me later. I had packed away the emotional remnants of those old issues and had brought my past with me as extra baggage—along with a whole list of "If onlys."

Through the years, this pattern of behavior seemed to be my natural modus operandi. I really believed that Shangri-La was just over the next hill, only to discover an empty valley on the other side. I eventually came to realize that before I could find and ultimately reside in Shangri-La, I had to find Shangri-La residing in me. What's more, I needed to take the time to unpack my bags before I could live there!

Unpack your suitcase!

As we navigate the twists and turns in that maze we call life, we make all kinds of choices. We decide where and how we will live, work, play, and spend our days and nights. We set priorities regarding our relationships and choose how and with whom we will spend our time. We establish careers, pick spouses, buy cars and houses. We also decide, or have it decided for us, whether or not we will bring children into the world. The operative word here is "decision."

The suffering comes when we continually second-guess decisions. We do this because we live under the misconception that the consequences of every decision we make are cast in stone, that they will never change, and that we will forever be slaves to their repercussions.

Although a decision may be considered a commitment—and it should be, or else it really can't be defined as a decision—the results manifested by the decisions we make do, and most certainly will, change at some point in time, because circumstances and our desires eventually change. Any decision we come to in our life could rarely be considered the end of the world; and if by chance the sun didn't rise the next day due to some galactic calamity or personal fatality, the decision we made the day before wouldn't matter anyway. In other words, any decision we make today will at some point in time be reevaluated and a new one will take its place. So, to sabotage our progress because we are afraid to make a wrong or right decision that will eventually change anyway is illogical and only serves to perpetuate the dead end effects of ambivalence.

I certainly didn't move enough to be classified as a gypsy or vagabond, but it was obvious to most people, including my husband, that I had quite a healthy taste for new adventures, new places and new experiences. However, I later discovered that some of what I defined as healthy curiosity was really an excuse that tended to obscure some much deeper issues.

First, as discussed earlier, I wasn't aware of the basic life principle that says you have to be happy on the inside before you can become happy on the outside. I believed that certain things "out there" would make me happy. Once I acquired a new career, a new house, a new and exciting place to live and (of course) enough financial abundance, then I would be happy! I didn't realize that happiness is a state of being, not a consequence of having.

In addition, I hadn't yet become conscious of the power of gratitude and I regularly ignored life's blessings. In other words, I wasted a lot of valuable time trying to attract happiness when all I had to do was decide to be happy with what I already had.

Then there were the unresolved issues related to my time in Florida that I was still dragging around with me. For instance, maybe I should have stayed in Florida and started my own real estate company instead of moving across country again. After all I had lived in Florida for 17 years, had acquired a lot of friends, and I really missed the sun, surf and sand. The real issue was that I had come to believe that all that was not perfect in my life now was somehow the result of poor choices I had made in the past. I reasoned that if I went back to Florida to visit, I could at least right some old wrongs, reverse some old, suspect choices, and maybe even move back to the beautiful tropics and start all over with a clean slate.

When I tried to share my thoughts with my husband, however, the idea went over like a lead balloon! The economy was slow, we were both between jobs, funds were low, gas prices were high and it was Christmas time, which only served to exasperate my husband more, since staying home for the holidays had always been a family tradition. After a couple of weeks and a number of less-than-cordial discussions, we finally agreed that we really didn't know what we didn't know, so we decided to gather up our two Pembroke Welsh Corgis, Tucker and Taylor, load up the motor home, and take a short trip back in time!

An emotional roller-coaster!

We weren't at all sure what we would find, but it wasn't even close to anything we could have imagined. After visiting some old friends in the northern part of Florida on Christmas Eve, we headed down to South Florida, which is where Bill and I met and started our life together. We took a tour down memory lane, walked the beaches, cruised our old neighborhood and visited some of our old haunts, but try as we might, it seemed impossible to feel at home again.

The area didn't look the same or sound the same, nor did it feel the same. Oh sure, I expected some change after all those years, but what I didn't expect was the level of unfamiliarity I was experiencing, and I was totally unprepared for the emotional turmoil that surged though my mind and body.

I realized that it wasn't what I was looking at that had changed; rather, it was who was looking. I was still the same person who used to live in the moment and make every day count; I just hadn't been acting like my childhood self for quite some time. At last I understood that I needed to look at my old stomping grounds with different eyes and, more importantly, with a renewed and updated perception of who I was.

What a change!

The two weeks Bill and I spent there were two of the most enlightening, enriching, healing, and growth-filled weeks of our life. We laughed and we cried, recalling old times and reminiscing about days long forgotten. Old regrets and packed away hidden emotional issues came up, came out, and were resolved for both of us individually, as well as between us as a couple. They seemed to evaporate into the cosmos, leaving us both in a state of awe and relief. We finally rolled out of town with renewed optimism about returning home. A heavy burden had been lifted from our shoulders.

It's true . . . you can't go back, but a revisit back in time is a great place to leave that old suitcase full of emotional baggage — and "If onlys!"

* * * * *

I've traveled far,
from East to West
searching for a home,
sat with friends
in crowed rooms
feeling so alone,
always moving forward
running from the past,
till one day a little bird told
the truth at last...
...Home is where the Heart is.
This was my Journey!

~ Author Unknown

Chapter Six Summary

You Don't Know What You Don't Know

- Being joyful on the inside is a prerequisite for experiencing happiness on the outside.
- It's impossible to fix the past but if you can recognize what was broken without trying to fix the unfixable, you will then be able to respond to present events effectively.
- By releasing old disempowering emotional perceptions of the past, we will be free to address the present and create a new beginning.

Self Coaching Questions. Your answers are only as good as the questions you ask! Here are some suggestions. Use a separate piece of paper to answer each question to determine if your perceptions and beliefs of the past still serve your today.

You Can't Go Back!

- What are your "If onlys?"
- What false perceptions are you carrying around about your past?
- What things can you do to disengage yourself from the past and move on into the present?

MAYBE NEXT WEEK

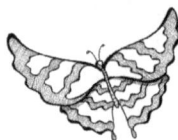

Friday adventures

Weeks always seem to pass so quickly. It's Friday again, which in our family translates to payday and grocery shopping time. My dad works nearby at Lufkin Rule, a factory that makes measuring devices. My parents only own one car so he walks home from work everyday, always commenting that he needs the exercise to stay in shape. On Fridays, my dad hands the check over to my mother, and immediately my mother and I are off and running on our weekly adventure.

We have so many stops to make prior to returning home for supper. Our first stop is First National Bank, a huge, red brick building which sits on a corner. When the check is cashed, my mother always counts the money over and over. I guess it's to make sure that she is given the proper amount or something. We then make Lawson & Lee Bakery our next stop.

I am not quite tall enough to see over the counter, but the smell of fresh hot bread, cookies and cakes would warm anyone's heart. My aunt Doris works behind the counter and she hands mom a hot loaf of homemade bread, fresh out of the oven. She also remembers to give me my regular weekly cookie, which I always look forward to. Right next door to the bakery is Vescio's Grocery Store. With newly clipped coupons bulging from her pocketbook, my mother quickly organizes her shopping list. We spend more time than you can imagine looking at all the wonderful goodies on each isle. I request a few favorites, but my mother's mood determines whether or not any of my favorites make it to the grocery cart. She reminds me that some of my choices are not healthy for me. Mom always stops at the cosmetics and beauty section. She ponders there for what seems to be hours, but I am sure it is only minutes in real time. I watch her as she admires bottles filled with wonderful smelling lotions and turns the rack of colorful lipsticks.

Before we arrive at the cash registers, my mother scans the checkout lines to see if one of her favorite cashiers is working today. We are ready to check out and the final items to be whisked down the conveyor go slowly. Item by item, my mother continues to ask the checkout lady what the new total is. As the total is given, the checkout gal adds items to the total that are still in the grocery cart, and upon direction from my mother, some items are held back that have already been scanned and ready to bag. Although it's always embarrassing to hold up the line every week, I guess mothers can change their minds, and maybe some of the things are not needed after all.

A tall gentleman wheels out the grocery cart for us. While he waits, we pick up the car and drive to the store's entrance and the bags are placed in the car.

We are finished with the major portion of our errands, but we still need to stop at Small's Meat Market and visit Parker Dairy for the freshly squeezed orange juice and local dairy milk. What a great day! It's always so much fun shopping with my mother, but I can't help feeling a little disappointed afterward. I will be prepared next week to convince my mother to add a couple of things that are on my favorite food list, or maybe I'll sneak a small bottle of bubble bath I have always wanted into the shopping cart.

Hmmm . . . I wonder what scent of bubble bath I will choose!

CHAPTER SEVEN

LET THE RABBIT GO!

One will never reach distant shores if he chooses to remain upon the dock in fear his little ship of dreams may be dashed against the rocks.

~ F. Bolen

False Evidence Appearing Real!

In some American Indian cultures, the rabbit is sometimes associated with fear, thus the title of this chapter. Fear is, without a doubt, the most crippling, paralyzing, and destructive emotion any of us will ever have to deal with. Yet by learning to transform our fear into total awareness, we can change this seemingly negative energy into one of our most positive allies.

Unfortunately, many of us are—as were my parents—programmed, to one degree or another, to fear or distrust anything we are unfamiliar with, regardless of any evidence to the contrary. It seems easier for most of us to accept false evidence as real rather than question it. Of course, appearance is the key word here since it is our perception of physical circumstances that unwittingly leads us to believe we are the victim of same.

Actually, if fear remained only an emotion, its destructive power would be substantially limited. It's when fear morphs us into a negative state of being and wraps its icy fingers around our heart and soul that it becomes a powerful negative force beyond description, preventing us from exercising our creative power and ultimately keeping our destiny at bay. Fear's best friends—anger, worry and doubt—work in unison to sabotage our efforts, allowing ambivalence to rule the day. We are either stopped cold or forced to act out of desperation instead of appreciation, and so we continue to suffer in regret.

Ghosts of the past

As I mentioned once before, regret was the ticking time bomb that was locked away in my emotional baggage, only to explode later when I thought I was ready to begin some exciting new life-changing venture. Frustrated and tired of trying to decide what I wanted to do with the rest of my life, I simply gave in, let go, stopped resisting and surrendered my fate to the silent cosmos, remembering that the more you resist something, the more it persists.

Then one day, during a quiet moment—when I least expected it—a voice penetrated the silence telling me I needed to write children's books. Surprised by this intuitive revelation, I was prompted to revisit my past again. As I thought it through, I recalled my mother having told me many, many times, "I know you'll be a great mother." I agreed with her, but time had passed so quickly, I hadn't allotted enough of it to be a mother and now it was past my time. Still endowed with a mother instinct, I wondered if there was another way I could contribute to the well-being of children collectively. It was then *Tucker Tales* was born!

I had adopted a beautiful Pembroke Welsh Corgi Puppy named Tucker, and I noticed the trials and tribulations he experienced growing up seemed to mirror similar experiences that human children went through.

What if I could tell Tucker's stories in a way that children could relate to? Maybe I could develop this idea into books that would be tools that would allow parents and children to interact and grow together. It didn't take me long to realize that this would allow me to live my life on purpose!

I spent hours, days, weeks and many months developing the concept, getting more excited as I created stories and collaborated with my husband. Then, for no apparent reason, fear and two other members of his gang—worry and doubt—showed up and shut me down. Ambivalence became the order of the day, rendering me incapable of making any meaningful or sustaining decisions. I had dreamed, planned, elicited help from others, even spent money to develop the ideas in words and pictures, but when it came time to pull the trigger, I froze.

First, there was the doubt. "How can I possibly make this work?" "Who do I think I am to believe I can do something so important with the meager resources and limited experience I have?"

Suddenly, obstacles were everywhere. Worry took over. "It's too risky." "I've never done anything like this before." "I can't possibly get my work published and don't even know how to begin."

Here was a really big one: "If this is such a great idea someone would have tried it by now!"

What made me so motivated, positive and optimistic one minute and so unsure the next? As I learned later, the ghostly voices of past regrets, conditioning and uncertainty about the future were creating fear in the present where it hadn't existed before.

Once more I found myself returning to my childhood for inspiration. When I was very young, my focus was on what I was experiencing at any given moment. I didn't consciously think about how I was going to accomplish anything, I just became so emotionally attached to my ideas that I took action and eventually found my way to success through trial and error.

Sure, I made mistakes along the way, but I was too excited about my goal to concern myself with them. I learned from my mistakes, of course, but as daily life closed in on me as a young adult and later as a married career woman, I forgot all about those exhilarating feelings I had as a child. Part of the reason for the lapse of memory was that society looked at such notions as childish or unrealistic. And I bought into it!

As I grew a little older, my mistakes were considered more serious. Family, friends, and even total strangers were quick to point them out. Having forgotten the truth about myself, I found I was paying more attention to my mistakes for fear of making one that might be considered irreversible.

By the time I was a so-called responsible adult, I was watching my every step and sometimes regretting my very existence when I missed one. Despite this negative programming, I managed to grow through my teens into adulthood and approach most things in a calm, rational and calculating way. I planned my days, weeks, and months setting goals and continually looking for new opportunities. There were ups and downs, setbacks and triumphs, but for the most part, I believed I was responding responsibly and appropriately to all the apparent obstacles and uncertainties life had to offer. I was enthusiastic about life in general, always ready to try something new; and if a calculated risk was warranted, no one could ever accuse me of being faint of heart.

As the years passed, however, I noticed a change in my behavior. I began to take an uncharacteristically conservative approach to these potential mistakes and their perceived consequences. It was barely noticeable and subtle at first, but little by little it was apparent I wasn't as spontaneous or enthusiastic as I once was. This growing malady seemed to come and go as I traveled through the various stages of my life but its progressive nature was noticeable enough to be of concern nonetheless. Bottom line: it was progressive and kept getting worse. The cumulative affect of this conflict made me feel like I had one foot on the accelerator of life and the other on the brake—and I was pushing on both at the same time.

The net result was I was less sure of myself and far less optimistic about the future. I felt guilty that I hadn't progressed far enough in my quest for perfection, and I still harbored resentment for anyone who I thought may have prevented or slowed my progress. I sometimes blamed others, but ultimately I was my own worst enemy. Just a little stored worry here and a little doubt sprinkled there had been enough over the years to finally manifest as new and paralyzing fears (false perceptions) that all but robbed me of my identity and prevented me from appreciating my divine, spontaneous, confident, loving, and creative soul.

The face of transition!

By the time I realized all this, I knew that I needed to fall back, regroup, and redirect my thoughts, goals and aspirations. As though by divine intervention, life forced me to confront my needs with ideas of its own. An old neck injury flared up and became a serious and debilitating condition that slowed me down to a crawl (sometimes literally). Since I didn't respond voluntarily, maybe this was the Universe's way to force a "time out." The two years I spent convalescing turned out to be a blessing in disguise. This extra time helped me wake up and realize the real truth in the phrase, "It's not how things look, but how you look at things, that counts."

This was the beginning of a transition for me.

A successful transition could be defined as the ultimate result of a personal transformation! A transition could begin with a loss of income or a financial gain, the loss of a loved one or the birth of a child. It could be a divorce or a new spouse. It might be a change of vocation or the sale of a house and the purchase of a new one. It could be as simple as changing your hairstyle and as sobering as facing a major health challenge. But whether you've just lost a loving pet or are experiencing the frustration of trying to figure out what you're going to do with the rest of your life, it still means that something is ending, something is beginning, and most importantly, something in between has to change. That something is *you*!

Every transition starts with accepting and understanding that the past does not equal the future, and the time has come to end one part of your life and to let it go. The logic here is that it's difficult—maybe impossible—to make a new start without first making space for it by finishing up and letting go of old business. Many people stall here and sometimes suffer for the rest of their lives because they fail to release old false identifications with self. Remember, your material possessions, the roles you have played, the things you have accomplished, your relationships, and your current ideas and beliefs are not who you are.

Release your brakes

I was struggling with my transition because I was attempting a new beginning without allowing an effective ending. I needed to transform my thinking to make room for the new, and that meant facing all those fearful negative emotions from the past and accepting the pain associated with the negative thoughts and feelings that the past had brought forward into the present.

But who the heck wants to do that? It hurts! And besides, all I really wanted was to feel better! It was a painful lesson, but I finally came to realize that no one can feel good about the past or the future unless they are able to accept the pain from the past and surrender to it in the present.

The biggest obstacle to such a strategy is that we as human beings will do just about anything to avoid discomfort and pain. Our entire sociological structure is geared to avoid pain through distraction and medication.

During my own transitional crisis, I visited my physician regarding an unrelated physical ailment. During my examination, I made the mistake of sharing my emotional frustration regarding my quest for the meaning of life, shedding a tear or two in the process. Don't get me wrong. I have great respect for doctors and their ability to assist healing. But doctors, as good as they may be, all too often can offer only medication, especially if there is no accurate diagnosis. After my doctor had patiently endured my concerns, she prescribed a sedative and sent me on my way. Now, I may have needed to calm down a tad, but I sure didn't need to slow down!

Again, this is not meant as criticism, just as a good example of our collective bias toward pain avoidance. As a society, we are plagued with all manner of escape mechanisms designed to numb our awareness, rendering us unconscious to anything that might be deemed uncomfortable. Alcoholism, drug abuse, eating disorders, obsessions with money, material indulgence, physical gratification, preoccupations with TV, cell phones, and computers, as well as cosmetic surgery are all efforts to change our exterior physical world while ignoring the realignment of our inner spiritual universe. The key to clearing the way for the new is surrender. This doesn't mean giving up on your goals, your hopes, or your ability to manifest an abundant and productive future; it simply means embracing the inevitable pain and accepting the negative feelings without compounding the discomfort of the event by getting emotional with your emotions.

There is an old saying that states, "This, too, shall pass." We all need to take the time required between the finish of the old and the start of the new. This is where the true personal transformation takes place. It's that "time out" in the middle that allows us to re-evaluate the event, let go of the past, adjust our perceptions of the transition itself, and project ourselves positively into the future.

When we have successfully made all the appropriate emotional adjustments and personal belief integrations, we can then make a meaningful transition into a new beginning with confidence and peace of mind.

There is another old saying that says, "Nothing is either good nor bad; only our perception makes it so."

Remember, a successful transition requires a personal transformation, but the experience does not have to be fear based and traumatic. Through awareness, surrender and acceptance, personal transformation can occur as gently and joyfully as we wish, depending upon our ability to adjust our perceptions of the event accordingly. Transitions are an evolutionary fact of life. But if we learn to release our emotional brakes, stay conscious, show up for the inevitable discomfort, and replace our fear with total awareness, any future fear-based suffering will be more the exception than the rule.

* * * * *

The only devils in the world are those running around in our own hearts – that is where the battle should be fought.

~ Mahatma Gandhi

Chapter 7 Summary

Let The Rabbit Go!

- Fear is a negative emotion that prevents us from exercising our creative power and ultimately keeps our destiny at bay.
- When a transition appears imminent, release your fear and turn it into appreciation and awareness by embracing the pain so that you may recognize it as just a feeling and not who you are; this will free you to address your transformation with clarity and optimism.
- Remember, nothing is good nor bad, only our perceptions make it so.

Self Coaching Questions. Your answers are only as good as the questions you ask! Here are some suggestions. Use a separate piece of paper to answer each question to determine if your perceptions and beliefs of the past still serve you today.

Scared Stiff!

- What are some ways you can transmute that scared feeling in the pit of your stomach into positive awareness?
- What areas in your life are you currently struggling with and need to change?
- What new stories can you create about the things you fear that will provide you with the courage to move forward?

CHAPTER EIGHT

WHAT DO YOU REALLY WANT?

I dream my painting, then I paint my dream.

~ Vincent Van Gogh

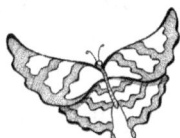

Deer in the headlights!

Have you ever watched what happens when people are asked, "What do you want out of life?" Generally, their eyes glaze over and they get that "deer in the headlights" look. Then they pause, looking this way and that, as if the answer is going to be found somewhere out there. Next, not wanting to give away the fact that they hadn't thought about it lately, most people proceed to recite a list of "stuff," none of which has anything to do with who they are or what they really want. In fact, more often than not the "stuff," they talk about tells you more about what they don't want than what they do want.

In all fairness, many people have been so caught up in the everyday responsibilities of life, they find themselves spending more time planning dinner than they do their lives.

When I was younger, if somebody had bothered to ask me what I wanted, I would have answered them without hesitation. Back then, I had a totally different perception of life. It was something to be experienced, to be participated in, to be embraced, savored, and celebrated. Of course, I wanted the "stuff," too, but my focus was mainly on the journey. Please don't misunderstand. I wanted to be wealthy, and I had enough confidence to believe I would be. But because I didn't totally understand the broader, spiritual, more complete concept of being wealthy, I was oblivious to the fact that I was already wealthy. I thought that wealth meant being financially well off. I didn't understand yet that wealth literally means "well-being."

I just knew I was enjoying the ride and life was good. As time went on, though, I started wondering where all that abundance was. Knowing I wasn't yet financially independent—and at the same time being totally unaware of my true wealth—everything I did became a means to an end. I totally forgot about the present and began focusing exclusively on the past and the future. Every day my perceptions changed a little, until the cumulative effect of being increasingly unable to appreciate my life began to take its toll. My heart was talking, but my ego wasn't letting me listen.

Stop, look and listen!

My husband, Bill, had taken on a new position in Santa Fe, New Mexico and one day, there we were living in a nice hacienda overlooking the beautiful Santo de Christo Mountains. Although I had taken a hiatus from my career and therefore had time to experience all the wonders, magic and beauty the area had to offer, our stay in Santa Fe proved to be one of the most challenging times in our life.

As I indicated previously, we had never gotten around to having children, but we did raise five wonderful and loving dogs: four Lhasa Apsos and one rescued Jack Russell Corgi mix named Tyler. Since their ages ranged from 15 to 20 years, you can imagine the effect on my state of emotional health when they each started making their final transitions, one after another. I loved all my "kids," but I had a particular affinity for Tyler. When he passed, I was literally devastated, and all the joy in my life seemed to evaporate. Already emotionally vulnerable from searching for my purpose in life, and now being overcome with grief, I simply became overwhelmed and stopped everything.

This sudden cessation of routine physical activity and everyday needless mind chatter actually served to calm my spirit. Since I had lost my ambition for everything and anything, I found myself sitting in silence quite often. I was emotionally exhausted and was suffering from a bad case of the blues. But this was a real turning point for me. I started seeing instead of just looking, and I began listening instead of simply hearing.

One night, while I was tossing and turning in a fitful sleep, a message came to me in the form of a vision. In my dream, I was looking for a house to buy and stopped in front of one and went inside. There, at the far side of a large vaulted family room, were two sets of double French doors that led out to a beautiful, tropical backyard and a swimming pool. My eyes widened when I saw my little dog, Tyler, lying down on the other side of the pool, framed by two palm trees. When I called his name, he came running into my arms and I instantly awoke—in tears. At the time, I didn't know that there might have been greater significance to the dream, but I knew the only thing I wanted at that point in my life was Tyler. Nothing else seemed to matter.

Soon after I had my dream, Bill's contract with his employer was coming to an end. Although I wanted to stay in the warmth and beauty of the Southwest, I was ready to move on from Santa Fe. We had previously visited Scottsdale, Arizona, and we had heard it was a great place to live, so I decided to look for a home there.

After five long days and looking at a few dozen possible homes, I was a bit frustrated and getting ready to call it quits, when I walked into a house that looked curiously familiar. It was like walking into my dream! It was the house I had envisioned weeks before in my dream! It wasn't just a similar home; it was the *exact* floor plan right down to the French doors and tropical backyard, palm trees, pool—everything! It was as if Tyler was telling me that to discover what I wanted in life and to reclaim my identity, I needed to come to this place. He was leading me to a sanctuary that would allow me to stop completely, look intently, and listen to my heart. I believed he was saying, "Rest here, rejuvenate, review your life, and re-discover Jamie." I still didn't know what I wanted, but I sensed this new environment would provide the opportunity to explore all the possibilities.

Get off the merry-go-round!

Although the Phoenix Valley is the fifth largest metro area in the country, Scottsdale is like a small town within a city. While the rest of the valley was mostly desert, Scottsdale is an oasis of green lawns and palm trees. I settled in quickly, decorating, getting accustomed to the area, and making new friends. But of course, I still wasn't settled in my mind.

For some reason, I had a difficult time finding consistent income. I became involved in real estate again, but I just wasn't as excited as before. I finally took a job with a real-estate related business, but I still couldn't seem to get enthusiastic about the position. I even began second-guessing the wisdom behind our decision to move to Scottsdale in the first place. I started taking trips to see if I had somehow overlooked that special place that would make me happy. On the other hand, this new area met all my personal criteria for a wonderful place to live. I enjoyed great friends, great culture, and great weather. So what was the problem?

One of the major issues was still centered around the loss of our beloved dogs. We still had Shana, our oldest Lhasa, but she was 21 years old, so we knew we would soon have to say our goodbyes.

Then one day we were asked by our neighbor to go on their behalf to the local pet shop and give them a second opinion about a puppy they were thinking about adopting. What a day that was!

During our visit, we were told that the puppy our neighbor had picked out had just been sold, but while we were there we discovered Tucker, a beautiful Pembroke Welsh Corgi, and it was love at first sight. We went back the next day, wrapped him in a red blanket, and took him home!

A year later, we also adopted Taylor, another Corgi, from a breeder in Southern Arizona. We were a family again, and that helped us move through the grief after we lost our beloved Shana. Our new family also helped me settle more easily and pleasantly into our new lifestyle, but I still felt something was amiss. I wasn't particularly excited about my job, I still wasn't completely comfortable with where we were living, and all the while the days of my life were flying by. Emotionally, I went around in circles, trading the ups and downs of my roller-coaster life for a merry-go-round. I was searching for meaning in my life, but without a direction or a destination. I was still asking questions like: "What is my purpose?" "Why am I here?" "How can I be of service to humanity?" Yet the answers to these questions remained elusive.

I didn't know who I was anymore, let alone know what I wanted. I was lost in a sea of uncertainty and drowning in an ocean of doubt and worry.

Think it, feel it, do it!

I decided I needed to refocus if I was ever going to get back on track. I committed to a year-long coaching program with Bob Proctor, one of the best personal development consultants in the business. I followed his curriculum religiously, reading, listening to tapes, watching DVDs, completing all the exercises, and participating in the required conference calls. I started to feel better about myself, adjusting my perceptions about things and taking action. Then out of the blue, I had a unique opportunity to meet Bob in person. He graciously invited my husband and me to meet him between engagements.

Suddenly, there we were, sitting across the table from him in a Las Vegas coffee shop. The meeting was brief but nonetheless profound. He leaned across the table, stared into my eyes and asked, "Jamie, what do you really want?" And then he waited for a reply.

I searched my brain for an intelligent response, but none came. That was when I realized I had missed one of the most important points of his program. If you don't have a good idea of what you want and—more importantly—why you want it, you will not have enough positive emotional motivation to take the action necessary to alter your present circumstances. It was time to go home, regroup and revisit my heart.

After I returned home and did a good deal of soul searching, I realized I was just trying too hard. I was trying to force circumstances, consuming myself with the *how* instead of taking the time to figure out *what* I really wanted and more importantly *why*.

I decided I had been doing plenty of asking but not near enough allowing. I reasoned that I could ask all I wanted, but I would never be able to receive the clarity I needed until I surrendered to the present and started allowing the spirit to flow through me.

I indulged in a myriad of activities during my trans-formational journey. These experiences sparked new growth, expanded my mind, and eased the pain of uncertainty. This helped me create better thoughts in order to enjoy each and every day. I was developing a personal prescription for well-being!

I created a vision board and began to visualize what I wanted my life to look like. I continued to build an extensive personal development library; I read dozens of books and listened to anything that was inspirational, motivational, or coaching-related. I invested in seminars whenever I had an opportunity, always looking for another nugget of wisdom to add to my inventory of principles to live by. I found most of this material enlightening and educational, and it all helped me stay focused. I filled my calendar with classes, workshops and networking events, and even completed a ten-week career coaching class.

In addition, I wrote myself a letter about how I would spend my perfect day if money and time were not factors. I supported the goals represented in my letter with daily affirmations. I became more active in my spiritual community, not only volunteering for projects that interested me but also tithing on a regular basis.

I continued my daily meditation, learned how to breathe properly, and began looking forward to that special time with my creative consciousness. I also began to pray regularly and consciously paid more attention to my thoughts, feelings and words.

I treated myself to all manner of relaxation oriented activities, including facials, bubble baths, massages, aroma therapy, and just sitting quietly, listening to soft music while sipping my favorite tea. I discontinued the local newspaper and all but turned off the TV, reserving it for inspiring films and personal development DVDs. I consciously decided to spend more time in nature, so I created a flower and herb garden, hung wind chimes to listen to, and placed hummingbird feeders so that I could watch nature at my doorstep.

I began a gratitude journal, and every night before bedtime I wrote my thanks for all that I perceived as good in my life. I started a Master Mind group of like-minded people and shared dreams and ideas. My house, car and office became organized, and I cleared out the old, making room for the new. I forged new friendships and expanded my circle of influence. I took the time to experience and feel every moment and began to appreciate life's little pleasures again, even if it was something as simple as enjoying an occasional ice cream cone. I enrolled in various classes that interested me, including art lessons, personality assessment training, yoga, feng shui, reiki, jewelry design and scarf painting.

I felt as though I was designing a "personal recipe" for a joyful life. The more I read and the more I relaxed, the closer I came to the *what* and *why*, and the better I was beginning to feel. Yet I still couldn't seem to get a clear vision of my future. I knew life was calling on me to expand, but the big *what* was still an elusive butterfly.

How do you know what you really want?

The challenge was to break my habit of trying to force and control changes in my circumstances on a physical level. I was still programmed to believe that money, age, education, where I was living, and any number of excuses were responsible for my circumstances and dictated my level of happiness. I really didn't have a clue as to how to engage my creative consciousness.

Intellectually, I understood the concept of manifesting through the divine source, but I later realized that my subconscious was programmed to believe otherwise and thus would sabotage any action that was to the contrary, regardless of how determined I was to move toward my goal. This pre-programmed "habit machine" was keeping me from identifying and fully clarifying my *what*. I had become an expert in searching, searching, searching — reminding my subconscious of my lack and manifesting more of the same.

It wasn't until I began to truly care about how I felt at every moment that I began to develop the deliberate intention to feel good. I monitored my feelings during every activity I engaged in. If I tried something new and it didn't feel good, I would adjust my thoughts or try something else until it did feel good. What did I have to lose? I decided I needed to stay in vibrational harmony with what I wanted to move toward and attract. If my thoughts and actions made me smile, then I must be on the right track; and if I felt like singing and dancing, I knew the *what* was just around the corner. The fact that I continued to keep trying new things and monitored the feelings along the way was key for me. Anyway, the worst that could happen was that I would have to find something new to feel good about. I was beginning to realize that the real purpose in anyone's life should be to feel good and be joyous!

When people are asked, "What do you want?" they generally answer by telling you what they *don't* want instead. This is okay as long as their attention switches immediately to what they really want. If it fails to do so, however, this pattern of answering a question with exactly the opposite of what you want will create vibrational harmony with what you don't want. This is because the subconscious may not be equipped to process the words *no*, *not*, or ***don't***. So if your answer to the question of happiness is "I don't want to be unhappy!" — guess what? — your subconscious may only hear "I want to be unhappy." Without realizing it, you are telling your subconscious "you want to be unhappy." It's interesting how a play on a few words can derail your objective and take you down a completely different path.

As Esther and Jerry Hicks share through the teachings of Abraham in their book, *Ask and It Is Given,* asking the opposite can sometimes help you identify what you want, especially if you're still having a difficult time finding an answer. In this case, you might ask yourself the negative question, "What *don't* I want?" That may help your mind to immediately focus on a better selection and a clearer picture of what you *do* want. Attach some sincere, positive emotion to that thought and you will begin identifying, moving toward, and attracting to you that which you really want.

Through exploration and some old-fashioned patience, and giving this new behavior enough time to become a habit, success will become the experience of the entire journey rather than just a destination. When I truly understood this concept, I stopped searching and started exploring. I found that the very act of searching for something was actually a negative activity because it was reminding my subconscious of something I was lacking or didn't have. When I began to explore and be truly aware of what was available to me, I started to experience the journey. I moved from a negatively-based intellectual perception to an action-based, heartfelt experience. Once you stop searching for a mental conceptualization of what you think you want, then you can let exploration provide an experience that will allow your creative consciousness to lead you to what you really want.

It felt as though I was waking up from a very long sleep. Although deep down I knew I still had some additional perceptual work to accomplish before I could move on, my heart was telling me I was finally back on the right track. I came to realize that the answers weren't out there, but they had always been within me, waiting to be experienced!

* * * * *

The biggest adventure you can ever take is to live the life of your dreams.

~ Oprah Winfrey

Chapter 8 Summary

What Do You Really Want?

- Listen to your heart instead of your head; monitor your feelings along the way.
- Meditate, take time to stop, look and listen, and allow the divine source to flow to and through you.
- Stop searching and start exploring; Searching is looking for something you don't have and therefore sets up a subconscious negative connotation; Exploring is an experiential activity that allows you to apply new knowledge thru trial and error, thus enhancing your ability to determine what you really want!
- Searching is a negative perception and exploring is a positive experience.
- Surrender and let go!

Self Coaching Questions. Your answers are only as good as the questions you ask! Here are some suggestions. Use a separate piece of paper to answer each question to determine if your perceptions and beliefs of the past still serve you today.

Ask, Allow & Receive!

- If time and money were not an issue, what would you do with your time and money?
- Think of how many ways you can get excited about "what" you believe it is you "want!"
- If you knew success was guaranteed, "what" would you do right now, today and, more importantly, "why?"

BROKEN HEARTS, EMPTY CARTS

Tears and a stuffed dog

The local newspaper headline reads: "Yankee's Grand Opening Today!" This catches my mother's eye. Before we leave to investigate the new store, my mother yells out, "Is there any gas in the car?" My dad replies, "You drove it last, I don't know!"

Before I know it, my mother and I are going off on another weekend adventure. While I wait for her to get ready, I overhear her call my Aunt Francis and she explains that a brand new large discount store filled with all sorts of things just opened in town today.

My aunt lives 11 miles away and the distance between us prevents us from seeing each other often. My aunt declines the invitation to join, so it's just my mom and I.

When we arrive, the parking lot is jam-packed. We circle and circle until a space is made available. I never saw anything like it. The store is huge! Immediately, we get a shopping cart and tour the store, going from one department to another.

Then I see it! I stop in my tracks! I am starting a new collection of stuffed dogs, which I have already made everyone aware of. This one is just the one for me and I can see him sitting on my bed at home! My mother is in the department right next door. I am able to reach high enough to pull this cute, furry, cuddly, brown dog down off the shelf. I say, "You are going home with me!" I quickly locate my mother with excitement in my eyes.

For some reason, my mother's reaction is not the same as mine. I become disappointed and tears are streaming down my face in the middle of the isle. Somehow, deep inside, I know I'm going to leave without my newfound dog friend. My mother, of course, recognizes my unhappiness and explains that she wasn't prepared to buy anything today. I receive a big hug, and somehow I feel a little better. Anyway, I am reminded that my birthday is just around the corner.

I guess I understand why my mother didn't want to spend the extra money for my stuffed dog, but I wasn't quite sure why we ended up with a completely empty shopping cart. During our ride home, I realize my birthday is still five months away.

And I want that dog sooo bad!

CHAPTER NINE

CATERPILLAR TO BUTTERFLY

*And the day came when the risk to remain
closed in a bud became more painful
than the risk it took to blossom.*

~ Anaïs Nin

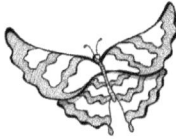

Cocoon!

I think we can all agree that change is inevitable. The face of our time continuum is in a constant state of flux. Nothing we observe on the physical plane stays the same. Some changes are so subtle and slow that we may not even notice them. Others come with such speed and force that they rock our world. The only thing that *stays the same* is change itself. This never-ending source of anxiety and uncertainty is perceived as a plague that continues to infect the human condition. Humans seem to have a natural propensity to resist change, but in reality it's a very necessary ingredient in our evolutionary growth.

Not unlike the caterpillar in nature, we traverse numerous transitions during our life's journey. We go through one change after another, ending one chapter in our emotional, mental and physical experience and beginning a new one.

If we take time to turn off the mind chatter and are quiet and listen, we can sense the approach of an impending transition. Our ability to handle change successfully will depend on our understanding, perception and level of awareness. All too often, we interpret that uneasy feeling in the pit of our stomach as fear, worry and doubt instead of a window of opportunity for personal growth and spiritual expansion.

As I was evolving from toddler to preschooler to teenager, I knew I would continue to grow out of whatever skin I was wearing. My transitions were so frequent, I didn't have time to do a lot of worrying about them. I no sooner went through one phase than I found myself starting another. There wasn't time to get mired down with *how* I was going to make a particular transition, since my personal transformations were almost automatic. My life's experiences during those years were constantly changing and growing, so it was easy for me to imagine that I could grow into or become anything or anyone I chose.

As an adult, however, I noticed my caterpillar facade took on more permanent characteristics. Circumstances lingered, giving rise to the false perception that this was all life would ever be. Like most people, I fought the idea. But as time wore on, my subconscious started to accept this perceived reality. Because friends, family and society seemed to subscribe to this physical picture of life, it was not difficult for me to follow suit and fall into the same conditioned intellectual trap.

People sometimes get so used to seeing a caterpillar in their bathroom mirror, they have a hard time acknowledging we are all meant to be butterflies! Of course, I spent most of my life consciously resisting this archaic and completely false identification with life, but the caterpillar was still there, in my subconscious, making a valiant effort to derail my aspirations at every turn. History shows I had made a number of successful transitions, but the older I became, the less effective I was at making complete transformations. I found myself languishing in the cocoon stage of my transition and refusing to let go of the caterpillar for fear that the butterfly in me, if it were there at all, may not grow wings.

I knew something exciting was beginning to happen, I could feel it. But after years of negative conditioning, I questioned whether I was up to the task. That old caterpillar consciousness was still buried deep inside me, and my attitude regarding its existence had allowed it to become stronger.

Lessons soon forgotten!

Astronomer-author Carl Sagan once said, "Absence of evidence is not evidence of absence." How quickly we forget! All I could see were the trees; the forest was invisible to me. I had concentrated so much on the misery associated with the appearance of negative things, I had failed to realize that I was responsible for creating my circumstances, positive or negative. Actually, my circumstances on that day did not mirror who I was in that moment. They were a manifestation of who I used to be. Michael Brown, in his book *The Presence Process,* states there can be quite a lengthy gestation period between cause and effect. When I began remembering all the wonderful things I had manifested and accomplished throughout my life, I realized I had always been the primary cause in every instance. I also had begun to understand that I was primarily responsible for the not-so-wonderful events as well. A great illustration of this is a quote from Jocelyn Davey's out-of-print 1958 novel, *Naked Villainy*: "Things don't happen to you; you happen to things."

This is a tough concept for many people to wrap their minds around, myself included. If we are honest with ourselves, we can all find evidence in our personal history that corroborates the link between our thoughts and the results they produced. However, when we translate this to, "We are what we think about," there is a tendency to question the validity of such a seemingly trite statement. Placing our attention on our intention is certainly a step in the right direction, but it's going to take more than just thinking to develop enough momentum to keep us moving toward our goals and dreams.

What is the missing ingredient? What takes a common thought and turns it into an inspirational, all consuming, mind-blowing vision that propels us into a life of fulfillment and joy? Have you thought of it yet? Can you "feel it" yet? That's right! It's "emotion." The word comes from a Latin root that translates "to emote" or "move toward." If what you want to have, do or be has a big enough reason connected to it (your "why"), you can't help but move toward your dream, providing your emotion is a deep, heartfelt feeling and not just an emotional reaction. You don't have to force yourself to take action, because positive emotions such as excitement, joy and a sense of well-being will automatically produce behavior that is consistent with your vision. You will become like a heat-seeking missile, discovering how to move toward your goal through trial and error. We often forget that this law works in reverse, as well. If the negative emotions of fear, worry and doubt become attached to our thoughts about our goals, we still find ourselves behaving in a manner consistent with our thoughts, but in this case we are inclined to take actions that ultimately bring forth results consistent with our negative emotions, unwanted circumstances, etc.

Self-made prison!

So there I was, in the middle (cocoon stage) of my transition, stuck in a jail cell of my own making. I was in a virtual no-man's land conducting my transitional battle. I felt I had waited too long to recognize my impending transition. I was not only physically incapacitated by the pain from my old injury, but I didn't know which way to turn and sensed I had lost my connection with spirit. I knew I needed something in my life that provided meaning, a sense of contribution and purpose, but I had no clue as to the *what* or *where*, let alone *how* to get there. I gazed in the bathroom mirror day after day hoping for a revelation, but none came. I wracked my brain trying to figure out what I wanted to do with the rest of my life, but I was locked in my own cocoon. The more I struggled to free myself, the more unyielding—and seemingly stronger—the walls of my prison became.

Finally, consumed by fatigue and despair, I stopped!

The constant mind chatter and the appearance of what I perceived as my reality were too much. In an effort to preserve my sanity, I totally surrendered to the moment and went silent.

It was during this continuous and repetitive meditative state that the first glimmer of clarity began to make its way into my now empty, quiet and receptive mind. Two new ideas came to me—with little or no fanfare—yet they had a euphoric effect on my spirit.

The first epiphany came when I remembered how much I had always enjoyed consulting, teaching and coaching. My most recent position, although real-estate related, had involved coaching. I helped agents improve their sales skills and develop their interpersonal acumen, and I also assisted them with career direction. I decided that if coaching worked for them, it might also benefit me, so I began looking for a personal coach I could resonate with and trust. Over the next several months, I conferred with a number of different personal coaches, each of whom excelled in specific areas of personal development. They appeared to be very patient, inspirational, and to have my best interests at heart. Some admitted they didn't have all the answers, but their overall knowledge and facilitation were instrumental in finding the right questions to ask. If you are able to find the one coach that meets all your needs, that's always the best way to go. Just remember, a good coach will help you draw out the answers from within your spirit.

My second epiphany came when I realized that although I was dedicated to successfully traversing this transition, I needed to let go and end my limiting perceptions of the past before I could allow and make room in my heart and mind for a new, empowering paradigm. In nature, this space in time is called the cocoon, or transformational stage. Intellectually, I wanted to escape my cocoon; but sub-consciously I was resisting change. I was stuck in the middle, unable to let go of the past and afraid of moving forward. The meditation techniques that taught me how to quiet my mind and end my resistance to change were literally a godsend. Becoming still and aware of the present helped me become one with the presence within. This facilitated the opportunity to listen to my inner spirit, which in turn informed me that I was again trying too hard. Although persistence had always served me well in the past, it became painfully apparent that trying to manipulate my transition interfered with the natural transformational process. In other words, I wasn't capable of making it happen. I had to allow it to unfold. The coaching, of course, helped me organize my plan of action and was instrumental in the rediscovery of past interests and desires. But I wasn't out of the woods yet!

Relief, release and patience

Society has taught us to believe that surrendering is giving up. The truth is, it's not necessary to give up to surrender, and where transformation is concerned, surrender you must.

Giving up is choosing to fail, but chances are you won't succeed or win at anything if you fail to surrender. To surrender is to accept and embrace all the emotional pain and discomfort associated with any transition. The old adage holds true here: "The more you resist, the more it persists."

When faced with transitional pain, many people look for relief and attempt to medicate themselves or simply try to hide in their cocoon. In nature, some cocoons never open, and the caterpillar lives out the rest of its days in a self-spun prison and eventually succumbs. The human condition isn't exempt from this. Many people who find themselves in the middle of a major transition spend most of their time searching for relief instead of exploring the experiential wonder of the change itself. They, too, find themselves wrapped in a cocoon of mediocrity and despair for the rest of their days.

Following our transitional metaphor of the caterpillar, the cocoon, and the butterfly, it's easy to recognize that there are three distinct parts to a transition: an ending to a current condition, a transformational period, and the beginning of a new opportunity. A meaningful and productive transition will be elusive at best unless a successful transformation results. Again, the transformational stage is the gap between the ending and the beginning, into which one must step in order facilitate their transition.

It took some time, but once I stepped in the gap, I was able to show up, embrace the discomfort, and then end what needed to end. I was able to stop identifying with the past and let it go. This release was the turning point for me. An authentic wave of relief washed over me as if a great burden had been lifted from my shoulders. I realized my old ideas about the past were not important anymore. Thoughts and beliefs about who I was, where I came from and where I was going no longer had any meaning for me. I was blissfully standing in the gap with nothing and loving every moment of it. No mind chatter, no anxiety and no concerns. I was comfortably alone, superbly conscious with all that I was; securely wrapped in my transformational cocoon, acutely aware of my breath and feeling the soulful beat of my heart. Patience became the order of the day. All at once I understood that my cocoon was no longer a prison, but my golden chariot to a new and wondrous life experience. It was time to let life unfold, to just let go and let God. Surrender was the key. Thank God, I hadn't given up!

Miraculous things happened when I was able to get rid of old stuff that no longer served me. First it created a vacuum. There is a natural law that tells us the Universe has an issue with voids. Simply put, the Universe will fill a vacuum with anything handy if somebody doesn't consciously restrict the process. Since I had freed myself of all my mental encumbrances, new and exciting insights and inspirations began flowing to me and through me, filling the void I had so intentionally created. They trickled in slowly at first and then the flood gates opened, allowing potential opportunities to flow in from all directions.

Breaking free!

I recalled hearing that clear vivid voice about writing children's books back in Santa Fe. I remembered when we moved to Arizona, my husband and I, in response to the voice I had heard, started to create a series of books based on basic growing up values like love, compassion, integrity, accountability, and other value-based ideas that children could easily learn and understand. During that time, I recalled the childlike feeling and excitement of joy and elation I experienced when I had worked on the Tucker Tales project. But because I was still resistant to change and in the throes of denial regarding my impending transition, I was having a tough time getting out of my own way, let alone getting out a book. So everything went on the back burner once again, looking like another passing fancy that would never see the light of day.

Can you imagine my surprise when *Tucker Tales*, my all-but-forgotten children's book series, again came flooding into my empty void like a tsunami from the South Pacific? Immediately, things began to happen with startling speed. I really didn't need to think much about *what* I needed to do or *how* I was going to do it. The habit of trying to manipulate my circumstances had ended and I had learned to surrender, and let the power of the divine creative consciousness take over. The vision was so strong, it truly took on a life of its own. Unencumbered by the old emotional baggage of the past, the momentum created by these inspired new emotions had me on auto pilot; and since I no longer had a past to get in the way, I found myself taking action long before I had consciously decided to do so, and the *how* of it all was at long last revealing itself. In the blink of an eye, new circumstances began to manifest themselves around my vision. You can call it the Law of Attraction, divine intervention, or anything you choose; but I can tell you that from that time on, new knowledge, people, contacts and all manner of resources came right out of the woodwork.

I began to feel myself growing, with the realization of endless possibilities. The walls of my cocoon were becoming tighter and tighter, threatening to burst open at any moment. I found myself acting like an author, talking like an author, looking like an author and knowing I was already the author I had always imagined. A new beginning was underway, and there was nothing I could do to stop it, even if I wanted to. I felt the restraints of my intellectual captivity weaken. My life was exquisitely unfolding as it was meant to, and I was emerging into a new and exciting beginning!

As the old emotional shackles of confinement released their grip and my cocoon fell away, I felt renewed, empowered and born again. My vision had become my reality, and my purpose was clear. I could see new horizons expanding before me, and I knew it wouldn't be long before I would spread my wings and fly like the beautiful butterfly I always knew I was!

* * * * *

We must change the way we change.

*Caterpillar to Butterfly: "How do you
become a butterfly?"
Butterfly: "You have to be willing to die."
Caterpillar: "Die?"
Butterfly: "Well, it feels like you're dying. But it really turns out
to be a transformation to something better."*

*When one door closes, another opens: but we often look so long and so
regretfully upon the closed door that we do not see the one which has
opened for us.*

~ Alexander Graham Bell

Prison

I'm in a prison,
I want to get out.
I shake the bars,
I scream and shout.

I think, if they come,
I will get free.
I will plead my case,
then they'll see.

I look at the walls,
I check the door.
I know I can get out,
I need to learn more.

If I knew how this
was built,
then I might trace
my path to freedom,
out of this place.

Alas, it was built too
strongly,
for me to break free,
For now I
understand,
It was built by me.

It's not made of
mortar,
or brick and of stone.
It's made of beliefs
I have accepted as
my own.

This prison of beliefs,
will hold me no
longer.
Knowing the Secret,
has made me
stronger.

I package them up,
and show them the
door.
They contain me not,
they hold me no
more.

Now that I know,
I'd be willing to bet,
I can leave this
prison,
without regret.

~ Curt Yeager

Chapter 9 Summary

Caterpillar to Butterfly

- A transition is a process consisting of an ending, a period of adjustment and a new beginning; some are major, others are minor in nature, but we all experience the pain and joy associated with these events at various times during our life's journey.
- The transformation is made during the time that is spent in the period of adjustment. This cocoon state between the ending and the new beginning provides sanctuary where one may transform their perception of the past to a new thought process for the future.
- This period of adjustment or cocoon stage provides the opportunity for reflection, re-adjustment and renewal and allows for a successful transition to a new beginning.
- Learning to quiet the mind chatter, by using meditation, allows one to neutralize the pain associated with past and present mis-identification. By providing a space for change through the "letting go" process and having the necessary patience to see the transformation culminate, you will have provided the best possible environment for a productive and fulfilling transition.
- Awareness is key, allowing yourself to transmute fear into awareness gives you an opportunity for growth and expansion and the best possible chance for an acceptable resolution.

Self Coaching Questions. *Your answers are only as good as the questions you ask! Here are some suggestions. Use a separate piece of paper to answer each question to determine if your perceptions and beliefs of the past still serve you today.*

About Face!

- What old perceptions and ideas about the past do you need to let go of to make room for what you want?
- What are some things that you can stop doing now that will give you the time to consider your new direction?
- What can you do to take your eyes off the closing door so you don't miss the new one that is opening?

CHAPTER TEN

RUNNING FREE!

As you're on your journey to success,
do remember to enjoy the trip.
Stick your head out of the car window,
just like a dog does,
and let the wind blow through your hair.

~ Peggy McColl

You've only just begun!

Whether we are age seven or seventy, our human nature would like us to believe that once something is fixed, it should stay that way. Our "take a pill for it" collective consciousness demands that everything that needs curing should be cured right now — and it should stay cured.

However, life repeatedly reminds us that with the exception of our true inner self, change itself is the only thing that doesn't change. This is because life itself is not a static thing, a fixed idea, or even a concept. It is an experience, and as such it must evolve, perpetuate and manifest continuously. Therefore, it is easy to understand that we must not only apply what we have learned to our current transitional circumstances, but we must also continue to practice and become skilled transformers as well. Since life is a continuous succession of transitions, the more we practice these skills, the better we will become at successfully navigating future transitions.

I consider myself to be a never-ending work in progress. Some days are smooth and others are rocky. I am not always listening and I don't always see. My decisions don't hit the mark every time, nor am I perpetually insightful.

It's true, life can occasionally be one miserable, gut-wrenching, anxious, painful drama after another. I have learned, however, that the more I read, feel, work to listen, and strive to see, life can also be a wonderful, provocative and joyous experience. For me, it depends a great deal on how I process events, what I identify with, and more importantly, how aware I am when I choose to think.

Here are some basic truths that have made a tremendous difference for me. I trust that these laws of life will enlighten and guide you on your journey as well.

Are we listening?

* * * * *

The intuitive mind is a sacred gift and the rational mind a faithful servant. We have created a society that honors the servant and has long forgotten the gift.

~ Albert Einstein

Many of our transitional experiences surprise us. They seem to materialize out of the blue in the form of a sudden layoff, a promotion at work, an accident, a financial gain or the proverbial act of God. Yet, there is a growing awareness suggesting that seemingly random events can be sensed long before their physical manifestation. Whether you accept this premise as truth, so much new age rhetoric, a sixth sense, or coincidence, we can all admit that intuition has played a significant part in many of our unexplained experiences. We continually receive all manner of intuitive messages in the form of heartfelt feelings, emotion, the written word, the spoken word, dreams, works of art, and musical compositions. We just don't always sense their presence.

I feel we are sent messages and clues constantly. I personally have experienced advanced intuitive thoughts that some might define as premonitions, but I didn't always take the time to stop long enough to listen! Some time ago, the sudden pain of an old injury forced me to realize that I was already in the middle of a transition. I had no choice; this unplanned event shocked me into stopping my world so that I could take the time to re-evaluate my life. Prior to this event, I let the drama, stress and demands of everyday life prevent me from being conscious of the transitional message my intuition was sending. If I had taken the time to stop and listen to my heart instead of conceptually analyzing what was in my head when I first noticed something amiss in my bathroom mirror, I could have avoided a great deal of unnecessary anxiety and moved through my transformation in a timelier fashion. Remember, you don't have to stop the world, you only need to stop *your* world so you can listen to your intuition!

Can you come out and play?

That which is the essence of us has been standing outside our door waiting to be let in. In our eagerness to grow up, we left our inner child behind, thinking that he or she was no longer needed. Despite our neglect, this divine presence has been a loyal follower through all our life's trials. Abandoned and alone, our inner child could only stand by, hoping that someday we would hear the insistent knocking at the door of our consciousness and open the portals of our heart once again.

It wasn't until I allowed myself to travel back in time and review my life that I was able to recognize the essence of my existence. All that I was or could ever be was locked forever in the spirit of my inner child, and I was the only one with the key. Once I was able to unlock all those old childhood memories, I found that all I had to do was invite my inner child back into my life and assure her that it was safe to come home again. It was then I rediscovered a clarity and focus I hadn't enjoyed since my Lemonade, Pickles and Worms days. Isn't it interesting how some things we enjoyed as a child stay with us throughout our adult life? Even today I still enjoy ice cream cones, hats, messy chili dogs, reading books — and I have an infinite love for animals and kids.

Let's be children again! Let's use our imagination, explore our dreams, play until the sun goes down, and awaken in the morning with the excitement, wonder and divine innocence of a newborn. When we can say, "This is the first day of the rest of my life," we can transform our mundane existence and set ourselves free. Once we re-teach ourselves to see through the eyes of our inner child, we will never again look at the world the same way.

Forgive yourself!

The idea of unconditional love is a difficult pill to swallow for many people. If someone betrays your trust, it's difficult enough to forgive them, let alone to love them without imposing any conditions at all on that love. Not many of us can do it. But until you master the art of unconditional love and forgiveness, you can never be truly free. Until you can love and forgive yourself and others with compassion, real freedom will continue to elude you.

We know that we can't forgive anyone else as long as we're dragging blame along behind us, and we can't forgive ourselves until we let go of the old self-talk stories we have accumulated over time. So why then do we waste our precious time blaming people, including ourselves, for everything? Why do we con-tinually carry around guilt, as so much extra baggage? It's obvious that the blame, guilt and the anger they generate are the most common reasons for not achieving a state of unconditional love in our lives.

When I was growing up, I felt that blaming myself was somehow nobler than blaming someone else. After all, I was reprimanding myself, wasn't I? That couldn't hurt anyone, could it? Actually, those instances of self-blame were more damaging than finding fault with someone else. The negative effect of personal guilt on self-esteem can be devastating and can last for a lifetime. The simple act of hiding my worm business from my girlfriends because they might think less of me probably had long-term implications that have prevented me from expressing myself openly and fully in adult situations.

Blame, like guilt, is born of fear. One or the other—and perhaps both—are at the root of many dysfunctional lives. Once we come to understand that fear is nothing more than "false evidence appearing real," or more precisely an excuse to avoid pain, we can let the rabbit go. And since blame and guilt serve no useful purpose, it's easy to see why we need to let them go as well.

The appropriate solution to fear is to respond through awareness. Fear is a negative emotion that can paralyze us and trigger an irrational reaction to an otherwise benign event. On the other hand, awareness allows us to respond rationally to the same event, thus giving us a better opportunity for a positive outcome.

But what do we do to neutralize the effects of guilt and blame? We are told that forgiveness is the antidote to the anxiety that blame and guilt create. So how do we resolve the negative repercussions that result from inappropriate behavior and achieve a condition of forgiveness? Maybe accountability is the answer!

Feeling guilty about doing something you weren't supposed to do, or vice versa, is not only spiritually debilitating, but it's a big waste of time, since it serves no purpose. Conversely, if you make yourself accountable, you might be able to take that wasted time and find a rational solution—or at least accept and admit to the pain of what is—and move on.

Blame is another irrational reaction that prevents us from solving current challenges. Accountability in this case means addressing the behavior, not the person. This allows you to intellectually hold someone accountable for their behavior by distinguishing between who they are and what they did. If that person decides to hold himself accountable, that's even better. But if he or she doesn't accept accountability, this approach still frees you to forgive and move on, since you are identifying with their behavior and not who they really are. In a best case scenario, it takes the negative emotion out of the equation and allows for a guilt-free resolution for all parties involved. By responding to events in our life with self-awareness and accountability instead of reacting with fear and blame, we can set ourselves free by forgiving both ourselves and anyone else involved in the interaction, and begin to work toward a better understanding of unconditional love for everybody.

But remember, forgiveness is a healing process that takes concerted effort and a certain amount of time. You'll know you have truly forgiven when you can recall the person or event without getting emotional about the original emotions and thoughts. You may still feel residual pain about the behavior that led to the event, but you won't compound the memory of the past with another reactive negative emotion by continuing to blame the person. You can then leave the past behind and make room for a brighter, more empowering new beginning.

Live life on purpose!

When you come to a fork in the road, take it.

~ Yogi Berra

* * * * *

Many people believe that life is God's gift to us. If that's so, our gift to God should be to live life well and love it unconditionally.

Some people believe they were put on this earth to perform a specific task and that their destiny is totally predetermined. Whatever you may choose to believe is a gift in and of it self. I feel we have the ability to choose to live a life by design or by default. Too many of us spend our life trying to determine our destiny and in the process miss our opportunity to truly live life and recognize the special gifts we were given.

I subjected myself to years of frustration and anxiety trying to decide what I was meant to do. My ambivalence prevented me from following up on some of my ideas and feelings because I was afraid I'd make the wrong choices and wouldn't like the consequences. I wasted so much of my time pondering the validity of a potential opportunity that I would either miss the opportunity all together, or I would eventually talk myself out of it. I didn't realize it wasn't *what* I chose as much as it was *why*. I have since learned that if I manifest an exciting idea, I should pursue it. My reasoning today is that if it hadn't been worthy of my consideration, it wouldn't have been given to me in the first place. The result is that at least I am moving my feet, using trial and error as a guide. Letting preconceived notions prevent me from taking action made no sense because I had no idea what new possibilities might be revealed during the process. You just don't know what you don't know!

Once we stop searching and begin to explore the journey we are experiencing, we discover that we don't have to find and unwrap our inner gifts; they will eventually reveal themselves and unfold their magnificent treasures before us!

If we are all individual parts of the same universe — thus making each of us a small segment of an infinite "one" — then perhaps we have more in common than we care to admit. Maybe we are not separate beings at all; rather, we are individual souls within a single divine whole. And if that's so, then perhaps we all share a similar universal purpose.

I feel being in a state of joy and feeling good is our life's purpose.

We each have our own interpretation of how we might demonstrate that purpose. We imagine what life would be like if we did this or accomplished that, and those visions help us pave the way to our perception of a predetermined destination. But regardless of the path we have chosen for the journey, let me suggest that we all share that same divine purpose. Whatever we accomplish in life — or aspire to, as each new day arrives — our well-being is contingent on our ability to make sure that each goal and each hope supports our individual and collective purpose, which is to love, laugh and live life to its fullest in joy, wonder and abundance. It's not something that leads us to joy, rather it's joy that leads us to that something that supports our joy. If we can find the presence of mind—which is to say that the physical, mental and emotional aspects of our being are in harmony with our purpose—we can live every day as if it was our last day on earth, and we should never again have to ask the question: "Is that all there is?"

THE ESSENCE OF DESTINY!

Choose your thoughts wisely, for they become feelings!
Monitor your feelings, for they become actions!
Mind your actions, for they become habits!
Study your habits, for they will become your character!
Develop your character, for it ultimately becomes your destiny!
In essence then, perhaps life is not bound
by the shackles of predetermined destiny,
but rather, on one's own God given freedom of choice!
The choice to laugh, love and live!

~ Author Unknown

* * * * *

Know thy truth!

Many of us believe that truth is something that's always right and never changes. But in the world we experience every day, truth is a relative thing, not an absolute.

When we refer to "truth" in a conversation, we are really referring to what we believe or believe in—and because it's about belief, we think that our truth is, or should be, true for everybody. Let's face it, for most of us a belief is nothing more than a thought we habitually think, over and over. Once we add a little emotional conviction to the mix, the thought is eventually programmed into our subconscious as "truth."

Since the original thought may or may not be based in truth, we could then find ourselves believing a lie. Beliefs are most often self-fulfilling prophecies that can be empowering or disempowering. The practical truth about all this is that believing is nothing more than the product of intellectual conceptualization and is therefore subject to change.

Authentic truth, on the other hand, is supported by faith. Rather than a thought process, faith manifests itself as an experience, often without any demonstrable evidence. It's an emotional, spiritually based "knowing" feeling, that transcends thought and may blossom into a deep-seated confidence that cannot be denied.

During the transformational stage of my latest transition, I was "Ye of little faith." I had so many erroneous, disempowering beliefs about who I was, where I came from and where I thought I should be going, that I found myself spinning my wheels, going nowhere fast. Once I was able to observe and reevaluate past events and circumstances with my heart, instead of a mental perception of memory—the reliability of which was dubious at best—I was able to identify and dissipate some old false truths about my past. My mind then quieted down enough so that I could listen to my inner spirit and continue my transformational journey with confidence, courage and renewed clarity.

Remind yourself that life is not a point in time, but a state of mind, body and soul collectively. Take the time necessary to meditate, listen to your heart, and let go of past disempowering, negative emotions that have spawned beliefs that no longer serve you. There is more than one path to your dreams. Expand your mind and dream big—so big that it's overwhelmingly exciting and yet scary at the same time. Let your cocoon unfold into a new beginning and watch your passion and enthusiasm take you to places you've never imagined. Relax, allow yourself to be present with the presence, and let your intuition—that heartfelt inner knowing—guide you to your truth. Then stand in front of that bathroom mirror again and listen to yourself ask, "Wow! Is that really me?"

Buried treasure!

It seems as though many of us spend our days and nights looking for the Holy Grail of life that will reveal the location of that buried treasure we have been so intent on finding. We search the far corners of the earth looking for clues that will lead us to that elusive quarry we call happiness.

There's an old fable about God holding a heavenly board of directors' meeting with the purpose of trying to decide where to hide the secret of life until such time that humanity was ready to employ its all-encompassing power responsibly. One of his disciples suggested a good hiding place might be the depths of the ocean, but it was decided that our insatiable thirst for knowledge and our penchant for ingenuity would result in the discovery of this coveted treasure too soon. Then someone proposed that the highest mountain might be a good place, and again the consensus of opinion was that we would eventually discover that hiding place as well. After hundreds of recommendations, it was decided that regardless of where they chose to hide this universal secret of the ages, there was no suitable hiding place that would keep humanity from prematurely locating this prize. Finally, after consideration deliberation, the heavenly chairman declared he would bury the treasure in a spot we would never think to look. It is said that from that day on humankind have been carrying that which we have spent centuries searching for within the treasure chest of our own heart.

This parable should remind us all of the undeniable truth that we don't find our resourcefulness, creativity, solutions, abundance, happiness, joy and peace of mind "out there." We develop the power that has always been within, and we take it with us wherever we go and into whatever we do.

It took a good portion of my life to figure this one out, but I finally realized I would never find happiness, joy, abundance or peace of mind "out there" until I found it in my heart first. I spent a lot of time looking for love in all the wrong places, when all I had to do was look within. I believed that the special relationship, the new glamorous career, the new business venture, or a new city or town to settle in would make me happy. Fortunately, I had found a very special relationship early in life. I think I connected with my husband, Bill, early because I intuitively understood the idea that I had to be my own best friend before I could be anyone else's. But I still needed to apply that perception of joy to everything else I thought I wanted. Without fully understanding the ramifications of my thinking, I found myself accomplishing one thing after another, only to find boredom and emptiness after the novelty wore off. I was setting myself up for failure because I believed all this "stuff" would make me happy. I had talked myself into believing that I'd be satisfied once I acquired this or that, lived here or there, or had enough money in the bank. It finally dawned on me during my transition that I had to discover my authentic joy within before I could be happy with anything else outside myself. Otherwise, I could spend the rest of my life waiting to be happy.

I started to become excited about my life after I transformed my perspective from searching for happiness to exploring the experiential joy of being happy. After that, every new and wonderful thing in my life served only to enhance the natural joy within me.

What do you think?

It's good for us all to remember that we have a choice. We can choose our state of mind from one minute to the next. The question is, "Do we really have the power to change our thoughts at will, thus allowing us to choose to feel good even when circumstances seem to indicate otherwise?" The answer is yes—as long as we understand that our thoughts had the major role in creating those circumstances in the first place. In other words, we have the power to change our lives just by changing the way we think and how we respond to events!

Our ability to be happy has a great deal to do with whether we believe we are victims of our circumstances, or we have faith that we actually create our circumstances. As for me, I choose to feel excited and empowered, which makes me feel good, because I know that the better I feel, the better chance I'll have to initiate the appropriate action that will ultimately manifest a reality that is consistent with my intention for joy.

When we choose a positive state of mind, we are choosing to feel good, and we are capable of doing this at will—providing we develop the attitude of gratitude. Happiness is not getting what you want, but wanting what you already have. When we appreciate our gifts, no matter how small, we set ourselves up to receive more abundance.

Regardless of how bleak the appearance of our perceived reality, there is always something to feel grateful for, if only the air we breathe. We know that the human brain can only consciously focus on one thing at a time. When we choose a single thought that empowers us, it's easy to understand that regardless of how much negative emotion might accompany a particular event, we have the power to divert our attention to something good in our life, thus giving us the best possible opportunity to reveal that good.

Appreciating the good in our life helps us to disengage from negative emotions and develop more empowering feelings that move us toward attitudes and actions that are more consistent with a positive outcome. This new awareness then allows us to respond to challenging events from a perspective of courage, abundance and renewal, instead of letting fear, feelings of lack and despair, and other negative thoughts and emotions condemn us to remaining trapped in who we don't want to be.

It's not what you want—but who you are!

We are given to understand you can't get what you want until you become that which you are. And you can't be that which you are until you decide to *be that which you want*. In other words, the minute you decide what you want to be, you must become that being in your mind, body and soul. At that point, it's time to stop wanting and start being that which you want.

Put on the costume of that which you wish to be, but leave the mask behind. Think, act, talk, dress, conduct your day as you see it in your mind's eye—but without the mask of false pretense— and your authentic, wonderful self will be revealed. Love yourself, demonstrate a deep gratitude for the abundance of life before you, have faith, knowing the divine power of the universe itself is yours, and you can't help but attract more of the same to you. Keep a daily gratitude journal and give thanks for this miracle we call life. Laugh often, for it is said that laughter is medicine for the soul. Give with your heart and receive with deep appreciation.

Life will throw us an occasional curveball and we may not hit a homer every time. But if we understand that we are all on the same team and remember to play our heart out, we may just discover that heaven is the journey and actually the ballgame itself, rather than a final score or destination!

* * * * *

Sing like no one is listening,
love like you've never been hurt,
dance like nobody's watching
and live like its heaven on earth.

~ Mark Twain

Chapter 10 Summary

Running Free!

- Life is a series of transitions!
- If you want it; you must first be it!
- The treasure is not outside, it's inside.
- Master the art of unconditional love and forgiveness.
- Allow your gifts to unfold from within.
- Authentic truth is supported by an all knowing faith.
- Whether you choose empowering or disempowering thoughts, they will ultimately affect your results in kind.
- Put on the costume but leave the mask behind.
- Listen to your intuition, run free and let your inner child lead the way!

Self Coaching Questions. Your answers are only as good as the questions you ask! Here are some suggestions. Use a separate piece of paper to answer each question to determine if your perceptions and beliefs of the past still serve you today.

Practice Makes Perfect!

- What are the things that you value most in your life today and are grateful for?
- Who besides yourself do you need to forgive? Learn to let go and let God!
- What truths support your present and will they in fact support your future?
- How must you act, feel and be to create your destiny?

CHILD'S PLAY – STORY #5

VACATION DREAMS

Volleyballs and badminton nets

Spring and school are coming to a close, and the heat and humidity of summer has made their arrival early this year. With my second year of school completed, now I can look forward to a summer of fun. I am thinking about how fortunate I am to have such good girlfriends that live within the same block. I am looking forward to playing with them all summer long. Just then, my dad arrives and is carrying a volleyball and badminton set that he just purchased at the local Hillier Hardware Store. I know we are in for some family fun and all my friends will be joining in as well.

A few days go by and my girlfriend across the street visits to say goodbye for several weeks. Her family decides to visit an aunt in West Virginia during summer vacation. Not only will I miss her, but she will miss out on all the backyard fun. Later on, the phone rings and it's for me! My special friend around the corner tells me that her parents have purchased a small summer cottage and they will be taking a summer vacation too. I won't see her again until late August—just in time for the new school year to start again.

I go to bed wondering how we can have fun with our new volleyball and badminton set without my favorite friends to play with. If everyone else is going on vacation with their family, maybe I should too.

In the morning, I decide to get the family's map out and start studying the U.S. for a possible family vacation. I know that if I can get away somewhere too, everything will be all right. As I sit down with my mom and dad, with vacation ideas and map in hand, they quickly remind me "vacations cost money and money doesn't grow on trees."

That night, I drift off to sleep holding the roadmap in my hands, dreaming of new and exciting adventures!

CHAPTER ELEVEN

FACES OF TRANSITION

For your eyes only!

My intention for this book has been to help people, from young adults to baby boomers, with their various transitional journeys. The goal was to provide a process, introduce some basic principles about why we, as human beings, respond to life's challenges the way we do, and establish a framework, using my story as an example, for a learning experience that you can participate in.

Although the story is a true and accurate portrayal of my personal encounters with transition, I'm sure we can agree that personal transitions are an ongoing fact of life, and there are as many different transformational experiences as there are people, each with its own unique set of circumstances. Therefore, I am profoundly pleased and appreciative to be able to present a collection of people from all walks of life who found themselves immersed in various stages of personal transition.

As I began my research for this chapter, I was both humbled and awed by the number of people who wanted to come forth and share some of their most personal, heartfelt and life-changing transitional experiences.

Although some of the authors of these autobiographical mini-stories indicated they have yet to realize a complete transformation, it seems many of the contributors have experienced an unexpected healing and inner peace just by putting pen to paper. I trust that you, too, will appreciate their contributions and come away with a new and expanded understanding of your own personal experience with past, present and future transitions.

It's the ability to view life through the eyes of others that sometimes helps us see ourselves!

Here are their stories.

Trisha's Story

Journeys With Jonah

It was a glorious summer day as my husband, Steve, and I walked along the harbor with Jonah, our Yellow Lab, leading the way. Passersby, wanting to say hello and pet his soft fur, stopped Jonah, who looked jaunty in his sky-blue bandana. He was happy to oblige, rewarding his admirers with wet kisses and a wagging tail. From out of nowhere, a large Dalmatian came trotting over, unleashed, with no owner in sight. Without warning, he suddenly lunged at Jonah and, with snarling teeth, viciously began attacking him. I screamed as the spotted dog bit Jonah on his face and snout, and patches of red began to stain his white fur. My husband jumped between them to break up the fight. It was all we could do to pull the Dalmatian off our gentle Lab, who apparently was not fighting back. Steve scooped Jonah up in his arms and we ran to the car to get him to the animal hospital.

When the vet explained there was no permanent damage and our Lab would make a full recovery, Steve and I both let out great sighs of relief, but our moment of consolation was short lived. We were told we had to go back and find the dog, and his owner, to make certain that his rabies shots were up to date. If we were unable to do so, Jonah would have to endure a series of painful shots.

My stomach churned as we made our way back to the harbor, and I silently prayed we would somehow find the Dalmatian again and that his shots would be current. As we got out of the car, my prayer was quickly answered, for there in the distance was the Dalmatian, standing alongside his owner. We explained what happened, and the owner apologized, assuring us that his dog was healthy. I was still wary of the spotted dog and was holding Jonah's leash extra tight, but he pulled and whimpered, and in one great tug he broke free. My heart froze as I envisioned another attack. I thought this time Jonah would fight back in retaliation and it would be a fight to the death. Instead, with his little face all bandaged up, Jonah looked at the Dalmatian—not with anger, fear, or even caution, but with loving eyes. He began nuzzling and licking the Dalmatian, as if to say, "That's okay. It doesn't hurt too much . . . I forgive you."

I couldn't believe it! In that moment, I had a profound realization: our canine friends are much more than pets or secondary beings that we love and take care of. If we take a step back and see them through "different eyes," we will see that they are really meant to be examples for *us*. I learned a great lesson in forgiveness that day and from then on saw Jonah in a different light. I started to observe the way he reacted to his surroundings and began my "apprenticeship," eager to learn the lessons he had to teach me. Lessons like "just be friendly and offer a smile to everybody you meet," "find joy in the simple pleasures of being outside in nature," and "just love unconditionally, without holding onto grudges."

The months that followed were a happy time for the three of us, as we set off on weekly adventures exploring quaint little towns along the California coast, with Jonah always leading the way. Then, one day, quite by accident, I made the discovery that no wife ever wants to make: Steve was having an affair.

The next few weeks were a blur, as Steve moved out to live on his sailboat. By then it was clear that Jonah was more my dog than Steve's, since he was never far from my side, so we shared custody of Jonah, with Steve taking him on weekends. It was good to have my loyal, furry friend there to comfort me through my tears, and his daily antics provided comic relief for my broken heart.

Since Steve, Jonah, and I had traveled the entire western coast together, I decided to write a book about traveling with a dog, thinking it might be a good way to put the drama of divorce behind me and move on. Jonah was to be on the front cover, so I made a grooming appointment for him prior to the photo shoot.

Steve had taken Jonah, as usual, for his weekend visitation and volunteered to drop him off at the appointment, which was scheduled for Monday morning.

On Monday, the phone rang. The groomer was calling to see what happened, as Jonah never showed up. The phone was next to my computer and I noticed an e-mail from Steve marked "important." I was shaky as I read his words, "Trisha . . . I have decided to keep Jonah permanently as I am really lonely and need him. I know you will be upset, but I don't care because I need to take care of myself now. I am sorry, but you will never see Jonah again."

As I stared at the words in disbelief, I began sobbing hysterically! I sat there in utter sorrow and pain, feeling as if my child had been kidnapped. I wondered how much more I could take. First I had lost my husband. But then to lose my precious dog and best friend who shared such a special bond with me! It was too much.

In the weeks and months that followed, I did everything to find Jonah and bring him back, but every lead led nowhere. Steve had disappeared, taking Jonah with him.

Every morning I would wake up thinking it was all a bad dream. Then I would catch a glimpse of Jonah's empty bed, and waves of grief would again wash over me. Thoughts of anger and revenge seemed to occupy my time, as I thought of the injustice done to me. The grief and bitterness I felt was affecting every part of my life.

Then, one day, I was taking a walk and happened to see a Dalmatian. Suddenly the memory of that traumatic summer day along the harbor returned, and I remembered Jonah's incredible act of forgiveness. If Jonah could forgive his attacker so graciously, even while bandaged and in pain, couldn't I follow Jonah's example and forgive Steve?

Tears began to well up as I realized how much Jonah had taught me in the six years I had with him and what a blessing he had been to my life. The hurt seemed to dissolve as my heart overflowed in gratitude to have been given the gift of knowing and loving this special little dog. My sweet Jonah loved everyone he ever met, and his irrepressible spirit delighted in all of God's creation. His whimsical daily antics did more than warm my heart and make me laugh—I learned how to live a happy, joyful life from his example.

Jonah was not only my pet, faithful companion, and best friend, but also he taught me one of the most powerful lessons of my life: the power of love and forgiveness. Thank you, Jonah . . . I love you.

* * * * *

Trisha Franklin went on to write down the stories and lessons she learned from Jonah, in the hopes of helping other folks who have suffered the heartbreak of losing a beloved pet from a broken relationship. You can find these powerful lessons and charming stories in her forthcoming book, Journeys With Jonah... A Dog Lover's Story of Love, Loss and Forgiveness. *www.JourneysWithJonah.com*

Maureen's Story

Left Behind

I hadn't been asleep that long. My husband and two sons had gone to a Super Bowl party that day and reminded me that if the game ended late they would stay over at my parents' home, so I decided to turn in, thinking they had done so. During the night, I awoke to a room glowing with light. I assumed it must be moonlight and drifted back to sleep. I would learn later that there was no moon that night.

It was 3 a.m. when I was again awakened, this time by a loud knock at the front door. I opened the door to the somber faces of two highway patrol officers. They proceeded to inform me that the loves of my life had been involved in an automobile crash. As they were driving home from the party, they were hit by a truck driven by a drunk driver and were killed.

My entire family had been taken from me and I had been left behind. That night, at 36 years of age, the world as I knew it came to an end.

As the weeks and months passed, the unbearable pain and torment evolved into anger. How could something like this be allowed to happen? How could God let this happen? The intense agony and loneliness would have numbed my soul and turned me into a recluse if I hadn't had the prayers and loving support of friends, family, and the community at large. I knew I needed time to reflect, pray and heal. I surrendered myself and began to pray and reflect—and then pray some more. With the help of psychotherapy and spiritual counseling, I started gaining clarity and strength.

As the years passed, I slowly began to emerge into a new beginning and a new understanding of myself. I was finally able to embrace the pain as something to be *experienced* rather than something to be *identified with*.

Holidays, birthdays, and old tunes from the past continue to trigger emotions and discomfort, but I am getting better at remembering to appreciate the gifts of love, joy, and laughter I had once shared with my wonderful family. We loved, laughed and cried together then, and we still do today, in spirit.

I know now that the glow in my room, earlier on the night I lost my family, was created by their spiritual presence. I believe they wanted one last visit before they continued on their journey, to let me know they would always be watching over me.

These days I spend my time as a massage therapist and a hospice volunteer, helping others with their grief. Although I am still evolving myself, I try to help people work through their grief by helping them move beyond the sadness and remember the joy that they once shared with their loved ones.

* * * * *

Jeanne's Story

They're Playing My Song!

I'm sitting at my desk at work, staring at my computer monitor, and all I can see is the blank screen of a less than full life.

For 23 years, I chose to stay in a career I wasn't passionate about. Somehow I felt I had sold my soul for the security of a paycheck and had very little to show for it—at least far less than the joy I had anticipated at this juncture in my life.

I had always loved music, enjoyed singing, and people seemed to appreciate what they heard. Yet here I was, stuck in front of a computer, feeling empty and unfulfilled. I had struggled with the idea of singing for a living, but the fear of not being able to contribute to my share of the household income always shocked me back into reality. I actually entertained the idea that if I was unable to support myself, my husband might well divorce me.

I began to wonder where such negative, irrational ideas could have come from. I loved my husband and I knew he loved me, yet I allowed this thought pattern to persist. I felt small, insecure, and not good enough at home, in social situations, and particularly at work. For some reason, I preferred to be seen and not heard. I think I believed I would be "banished from the kingdom" if I ever thought about speaking my mind. Something always told me I should keep my mouth shut!

In an attempt to make sense of my life, I attended a class that was created to assist people in achieving positive and permanent shifts in their lives. The facilitator explained that the human mind is basically a "meaning making machine," and that the meaning we give to past events in our lives has a profound effect on determining how we respond to present day events. Naturally, I started to wonder if there was anything in my past that might be triggering some of my current disempowering perceptions.

While I was in this thought pattern, I remembered something that happened when I was six years old. I was in the hospital recovering from tonsil surgery, when I awoke in the middle of the night. I was in pain, in strange, dark surroundings, and my mother had already left for home. Scared and confused, I began to cry for my mom. The response to my cries of anguish was immediate and abrupt. The nurse on duty stormed into my room and proceeded to admonish me for my inconsiderate and selfish behavior. After she had finished her tirade, she growled, "Shut up and be quiet!" She then swooped out of the room on the broom she came in on and disappeared. I was so terrified, I was stunned into silence, and for the rest of my convalescence couldn't bring myself to express any of my needs.

This horrific memory provided just the epiphany I needed to get through my transition. I reasoned that the childhood trauma I experienced in the hospital had quite possibly programmed my subconscious into believing that my needs weren't important. Since I felt alone and vulnerable during this event, I also developed an unreasonable fear of being abandoned in my adult life.

This new understanding allowed me to transform my life. Once I was able to identify the childhood cause of my current limiting behavior, I could eventually eliminate its effect in the present.

Today I'm happy to report that I not only wake up in the morning with passion, but I also make a profound difference in others' lives by sharing my love of music. I am now a fulltime singer, songwriter and recording artist! I own a business and perform as one of The JaJa's (say it as "The Ya-Ya's") with my best friend Barbara. We market a new genre of positive and inspirational music that we distribute all over the United States and Canada.

Incidentally, my husband didn't divorce me. He's my most devoted supporter!

* * * * *

Jeanne Mac Laughlin is an inspirational singer, songwriter and recording artist and touches the hearts of her audiences through her music.

Ron's Story

Lady Blue

Having been a proud member of the United States Marine Corps during my young adult years, I had always considered myself confident and self-sufficient in my civilian career and family life. That suddenly changed when I decided to retire in 1999.

Like so many other new retirees, I had identified with work most of my life. I suddenly felt empty, alone and without direction. I had a good family life and I loved my wife, but she was still working; and since I was home alone most of the time, I found little to do but stare into the mirror, wondering where my life had gone. Although I made a valiant attempt to keep busy, I soon fell into a depression.

My wife and I had always been animal lovers, so we decided to add a new dog to the family, thinking this might offset the sting of loneliness I was experiencing at the time. We adopted a beautiful little cattle dog which we named Lady Blue. My transformation was almost immediate! Lady Blue and I became inseparable. We went everywhere together, from errands to camping trips. She became my constant companion. We played together, worked around the house together, and every night she would jump on the bed and give me an appreciative lick on the cheek before falling asleep.

For seven years Lady Blue was my life. Then, one heartbreaking evening, Blue jumped on the bed, gave me her goodnight kiss, and went to sleep, never to awaken again. For the next several days, my wife and I could hardly speak, and when we did it often turned into drama and tears. We both questioned our mortality, and my devastation was so profound, I wasn't sure I could go on.

Then one day my wife beckoned me to the back yard and insisted I gaze into the heavens. The clouds had formed a heavenly image of my little Blue, and she was staring down at us as if to say, "I'm okay, and I will always be with you!" After my wife and I wiped the tears from our eyes, I knew I needed to find some relief for my aching heart.

I looked for solace in every religious denomination I could find, but to no avail. My pleadings for spiritual understanding seemed to fall on deaf ears, since conventional religious wisdom suggested that animals had no souls and that I should "just get over it." Of course, none of this did anything for my soul—until I found Donna Rae Yuritic, an animal chaplain. Donna counseled me and helped me find some meaning in my suffering. She also directed me to a church in our area called New Vision Center for Spiritual Living. I became involved in their Animal Kinship Ministry and spent a good deal of my time with various animal rescue groups.

I have come to realize I am still in the middle of my retirement transition. I had identified with my job for so long, and then my beautiful Blue, that I had forgotten who I was. I am now in the process of getting back in touch with my authentic self. Through my Animal Kinship activities and my commitment to the exploration of my personal creative source, I can work on ending the negative perceptions of the past so I can make room for the positive reality of my new beginning. I know my transformation will be complete when I can smile on the past with gratitude, knowing Lady Blue's spirit will always be with me and that I can look forward to the future with heartfelt appreciation and joy.

* * * * *

If there are no dogs in heaven, then when I die
I want to go where they went.

~ Will Rogers

* * * * *

Ron Ogden currently devotes the majority of his time to fulfilling his life's purpose: assisting people during their grief process after the loss of a loving animal companion. Ron takes a strong stance against testing on animals and continually seeks tougher laws for the betterment and protection of all God's creatures. Currently he is an active contributor to the New Hope Cattle Dog Rescue Group, the Humane Society and the Animal Kinship Ministry.

Linda's Story

One Life, Five Beginnings

I began my life's journey in Mexico. I enjoyed a relatively normal childhood up until age nine. I was alert, bright, curious and a fast learner. I did well in school and I was an "A" student, but it wasn't long before I outgrew the slow-paced curriculum. Bored with the lesson material and my teachers, by the time I reached the third grade, I decided I'd had enough and quit school.

Transition One

I didn't realize it then, but I had begun my first major transition. I started babysitting and doing odd jobs, so I always had money in my pocket—unlike most of my friends, who were still in school. The challenge was that when I was available for fun, they were in school, and when they were available, I was working. As the years went by, I also noticed that my friends had reached a certain level of educated sophistication. I not only felt left out of the whole process of growing up, but I was beginning to realize the importance an education played in being able to grow and prosper. That was my first transformational lesson. Although I had learned that decisions should be made promptly with conviction, and are changed slowly if at all, I also learned one must monitor the results and that there is no decision that can't be changed when necessary. So after being away from school for over two years, I re-enrolled and went on to finish high school.

Transition Two

When I was 18, I met a Mexican boy who visited regularly but had been living in California. When we decided to get married, I went with him to California and became pregnant with my first child. Talk about transition! Although my husband had lived in the U.S., he was very much a macho Mexican from the old school. He believed that a woman's place was in the kitchen, barefoot and pregnant. I dreamt of going back to school to get a business degree, building a successful career, making lots of money and living happily ever after. Unfortunately, before I had a chance to argue for my rights, my mother fell ill, and I temporarily moved back to Mexico by myself to take care of her. After she passed six months later, I rejoined my husband and promptly became pregnant with my second child.

Shortly thereafter, my husband decided he didn't want to raise kids in the U.S. and made plans to move back to Mexico. Fortunately, I was able to talk him into allowing me to attend beauty college before we left. When we returned to Mexico, I opened a small salon and quickly became the talk of the town, and financially successful as well. When I began making more money than my husband, it was the beginning of the end for us. He developed a penchant for young girls and drugs, drained our bank account, transferred our property into his name, and disappeared.

Transition Three

Since I was now a single mom and salon owner, the social stigma in Mexico associated with such a situation prevented the married patrons from returning to my shop. My thriving business was a business no more. I gathered up my two kids and decided to move to the U.S. I arrived in California with the equivalent of 500 dollars in pesos in my pocket, two kids in tow, no job, and marginal English language skills. Again I found myself in the process of transformation, and transform I did. I found a studio apartment, bought an old clunker of a car and took a job as a beautician in a high-volume salon doing 25 to 30 cuts a day. My goals were clear. I wanted a degree in business administration, a big beautiful home, a nice car, and a business of my own. I was tempted to say, "I can't get there from here!" But in my heart I knew better. Besides, I had an example to set for my children!

A year later, a friend agreed to loan me enough money for a down payment on an existing owner-operator beauty shop. With $4,000 in my pocket, the seller carried the balance, and I was back in business once again. After a short time, I had more business than I could handle on my own, so I took a big gamble and began hiring hairdressers at an hourly wage instead of on commission. I had converted my mom-and-pop shop into a high volume operation similar to the one I had worked for. Six months later, I added another shop, and then another, until I had a whole chain of shops and in two years went from $25,000 in gross revenues to nearly three quarters of a million dollars, which in those days was a nice piece of change. I had again successfully accomplished a major transition and completely transformed my life in the process.

Transition Four

Life was good and I was living the American dream, but I still hadn't made time for my degree. Then I met my second husband and my education went on hold once more. I had now entered yet another transitional period in my life.

This man came from a well-to-do family and was doing quite well in his own right. We finally married. I sold my shops, had another baby, and decided to be a wife and mom again. I found time to go back to school, and at long last secured my degree. However, my husband didn't see any need for me to pursue anything outside the home. But since I had been a successful business woman for so long, I felt my talents and opportunities were being restricted once again. In the meantime, his family's social obligations seemed to demand more and more of his attention; plus, his ardor seemed to be cooling off. After a few years of this, we drifted apart, eventually divorced, and I moved to Arizona to pursue my dreams.

Because I had signed a prenuptial agreement when I married my second husband, I found myself on my own again without any visible means of support.

Transition Five

I had to start all over and decided there might be some opportunity in real estate. Although I noticed that real estate agents were doing quite well at the time, their income was still well below what I had become used to earning. So, true to form, instead of playing it safe and becoming an agent, I scrapped together some money my ex-husband and I had made on some investments before our divorce. I took another calculated leap of faith and invested most of the funds into an old 12-unit apartment complex. It was touch and go for awhile, but I continued to put rental revenues back into the property and with the help of inflation, patience and a lot of perseverance, I sold that property at a substantial profit and continued to invest in commercial and residential real estate.

I now have a beautiful 6,500 square foot home, nice cars, a thriving business, two grown children, and one teenager. I believe life is made up of multiple transitions. Some include successful personal transformations, others are ongoing. Some transitions are born within, and others come from the outside like lightning bolts from the blue. Whatever the source, I have learned they all must be accepted and eventually dealt with. In reality, we never truly know what consequences our perceptions and decisions will produce until a result is realized. In my case, I was never consciously concerned about the "how" of anything. I was so emotionally involved in the journey, and trusted that the right path to take would reveal itself, that I always reached my destination.

If today was my last day on earth, my only regret would be that I hadn't dreamed bigger!

* * * * *

Linda Ayala is president and CEO of Ayala Properties, a real estate investment firm in Arizona, specializing in the acquisition and management of commercial retail centers, apartment complexes and single family residential properties.

Pierce's Story

A Change of Plans

I was in my late 50s, in the process of putting the finishing touches on what I thought would be my last few professional years and beginning to map out my retirement plans. Having enjoyed a long and productive professional career that frequently took me to the four corners of the world, I wasn't particularly eager to retire just yet. Blessed with a wonderful and adoring wife, I was in good health and found myself looking forward to the second half of an already fulfilling life.

My odyssey began with a nagging headache that lasted at least a couple of days. After a day or two of continuing discomfort, I awoke in the middle of the night in blinding, nauseating pain. It was obvious this was no ordinary headache. My wife called the paramedics, who transported me to our local emergency room and then immediately air-lifted me to another hospital where specialists were waiting. It was a stroke — and it would change my life!

It was touch and go for a while, but I was finally released to the care of my wife and allowed to return home. Initially, recovery was slow, and rehabilitation took a lot of energy and a great deal of perseverance. Fortunately for me, having a very hard working, cooperative, unremittingly insistent and dedicated wife made all the difference. This, coupled with my personal stubbornness, determination and tenacity, created a recipe for eventual recovery, but not without occasional setbacks.

The biggest challenge was coming to the realization that my life as I knew it had dramatically changed. I tried to return to work on a temporary basis, only to find that my place of employment had changed even more than I had. Although my employer of many years seemed appreciative of my return, office politics created a strategic impasse that was impossible for me to overlook. Once I resigned and returned home, the stark reality that I was truly in the middle of a transition began to set in. I knew it was time to let go of the past and begin anew.

Navigating through a life-changing transition is, in many ways, like waking up one morning and finding you've lost an arm during the night; nothing can be done about *what is* because it just *is*. Transition for me meant taking the time to evaluate and reorganize my perception of reality.

I have become involved in a good deal of meaningful volunteer work in my community, where my efforts are constantly being welcomed by those I help, while at the same time I am filling my days with purpose and meaning. In some ways, I am still going through a transformation, as we all do when we attempt to adapt to new circumstances and a new lifestyle. But I understand that when one door closes, another opens.

The secret is to take your eyes off the closing door so you don't miss seeing the one that's opening!

* * * * *

Note: This writer has elected to use an assumed name.

Cari's Story

Reunion

My parents were drug addicts. They were teenagers, barely young adults themselves, when I was born, ill-equipped to take care of themselves, let alone to nurture and raise a child. I never had an opportunity to know my dad.

For a time, I lived with my grandmother, until she passed away—and then I was again thrust into my mother's chaotic environment. Her world was violent, depressing and stressful. I know now my mother loved and cared for me as much as she could, but from my vantage point as her little girl, all I could see was a selfish, uncaring, irrational drama queen who seemed interested only in her next fix or her next drink. I felt unloved, dejected and abandoned.

Finally, at age 15, I reached my threshold. Although I didn't understand the concept at the time, I was ready to make my first major life's transition. I told my mother that I couldn't stand by and watch her destroy her life, nor could I continue to jeopardize my future. I told her that I was leaving, and if she was interested in a real mother-daughter relationship, she would have to give up her vices and clean up her act. Needless to say, our parting was less than amicable and ended in a dramatic, physically violent scene.

Over the next 25 years, I built a career, married a nurturing, loving man, and I have a wonderful son. I thought I had created a new life for myself, and I had. But something was still gnawing at my soul! I realized, after committing to my faith and undertaking some spiritual counseling and forgiveness work, that I hadn't made peace with my past. I had created a new beginning, but I hadn't completely released my anger, sadness and resentment. I was still holding onto the old, unresolved emotional issue of abandonment and all the negativity associated with it.

In December of 2007, I hired a private investigator to locate my mother to determine if we could create a new relationship. When I finally made contact, she seemed happy to hear from me and told me she had overcome her substance abuse. We talked on the phone everyday. We never talked about the past, choosing instead to be in the "now."

Our renewed relationship seemed happy, sweet and positive, until she and her husband came to visit me in February of 2008 and I discovered she was still a heavy drinker. She had lied to me. Although I was again disappointed, I realized that I had to make a critical choice—love her, or again end our relationship. Could I accept her just the way she was? If my new beginning was to be all I wanted it to be, I needed to let go and completely end the pain, resentment and unwarranted guilt I was still carrying around with me. With the help and guidance of my spiritual practitioner and my minister, I chose forgiveness, and I chose to love my mother and myself unconditionally.

At that moment, I ended my preoccupation with the past, which left plenty of room in my heart for a new beginning and the opportunity to experience a new, intense feeling of gratitude for where I am, where I am going, and who I am becoming.

Seven months after our reunion, my mother passed away from the residual effects of her hard life. I was grateful to have been able to reconnect with her and spend what little time she had left together.

After her passing, I felt like I had been abandoned all over again. Although I am still dealing with the emptiness of her absence, I have learned that forgiveness and gratitude can help me get through anything. I am placing my attention on choosing to relive the positive aspects of our relationship. I know I am a stronger person for having had this experience and I am deeply grateful to my mother for teaching me to release judgment and to love unconditionally.

Love does really conquer all!

* * * * *

Cari Vasicek

Wayne's Story

Running For My Life!

As a kid, I was always a bit overweight. I remember that in school I was taller and heavier than most of the other boys in my class. In college, my weight was somewhat above average for my height of 6'1", but I never thought of myself as fat. After I married, I began gaining weight but didn't give it much thought. Growing up in Minnesota in the '50s and '60s, eating a typical Midwest diet, contributed to the weight gain. During college, I began smoking cigarettes. During the '60s, everyone was smoking, so it was *the* thing to do to be part of the in-crowd. The smoking, I rationalized, would keep my weight down. I actually lost some weight during the years I smoked.

In early 1970, I moved from Minneapolis to Phoenix. As a result of the move and other reasons, my wife and I decided to divorce. During the time my marriage was failing, I had numerous bouts of pneumonia, congestive lung disorders, sinus infections, and other upper respiratory problems. My doctor kept telling me that if I quit smoking, my respiratory problems would likely go away. His encouragement, along with reading many of the reports about what smoking does to the human body, led to my decision to quit. As I found out, it was easier said than done; and after trying many tapering-off programs, I decided that the best way was to just quit! One day at a time, and with a lot of support from friends and relatives, I was smoke-free for one month, then two, then six. Finally, I considered myself completely cured of smoking.

As a trade-off for quitting, I began putting on weight. My waist size went from 34" to 36," and finally to 38." As my wardrobe changed, I began to feel uncomfortable in my body. I thought, "If I was able to stop smoking, I can surely lose weight as well."

I began studying weight loss, reading everything I could get my hands on. What I read pointed to two main factors to control my weight: diet and exercise. I studied what foods would be best for weight loss. I also read about what exercises would help with taking off weight. One of the studies showed the amount of calories burned for each type of exercise. Running was the highest in terms of calories burned per hour. Being a type A personality, I decided that running was what I would do, since I wanted quick results and I wanted them now!

I found that running was a simple exercise requiring no special equipment other than good running shoes. I began my regimen by trying to run around the block. The first time, I didn't make a quarter of a block! But I persisted, kept my focus on my intended goal, and each day found that I could go a bit farther. A few months later, I was running two miles, then three.

Some of the other runners I met inspired me to sign up to run a 10K race. Upon finishing my first 10K, I realized that I was hooked on running. The pounds kept coming off and I felt great! I loved running.

The good news is I lost about 70 pounds, dropping from 240 to 170. My blood pressure is normal, and my resting heart rate is low. Even better, I feel great, look great, and have a positive attitude about myself.

Today I am a firm believer that if you change your thoughts, you can change your life! I am living proof that this works.

Over the years, I have run 32 marathons, two ultra-marathons, and countless half-marathons and 10K races. My best time for a marathon was 3:16:40 at the Avenue of Giants Marathon in Northern California, and my toughest run was Pike's Peak in Colorado.

Then one day, my penchant for running created a most unlikely fringe benefit. As I was running a marathon from the North Rim of the Grand Canyon to the South Rim I happened to meet a beautiful woman named Donnita who was backpacking on the same trail. We met at Ribbon Falls, a spectacular waterfall at the bottom of the canyon. Six months later, our paths crossed a second time, as I was doing a training run up Piestewa Peak in Phoenix, and Donnita was again hiking on the same trail.

Well, the rest is history, but that isn't the end of the story. On our honeymoon in Hawaii, we designed a business plan that would further change both our lives. For the past 22 years of our marriage, we have parlayed my love of running, her fondness for hiking, and our mutual interest in travel into a successful tour operation. Our business, Open Road Tours, offers sightseeing and adventure tours from Phoenix, Sedona and Flagstaff. If you think I'll ever stop running, think again!

Our lives have moved forward on a wonderful path over the years, all because of our commitment to change our thoughts, focus on our dreams, and listen to the inner voice that guides us through our days.

* * * * *

Wayne and Donnita Parker are owners of Open Road Tours in Arizona. Their love for travel and the great outdoors has taken them on many exciting adventures together as they continue to share their travel knowledge with other adventure seekers. Visit their websites at:

http://www.openroadtours.com
http://www.traveltothewest.com
http://www.travelthesouthwest.com
http://www.experientialjourneys.com

Kitty's Story

Expect The Unexpected

It couldn't be happening to me! I had done everything right, hadn't I? I had a good college education, had worked hard, and had a good job. But there I was, with not one, not two, but three layoffs behind me!

Something wasn't working. I was 58 years old and still asking, "What should I be when I grow up?" Maybe I was asking the wrong question. Perhaps a more meaningful question would have been, "What do I want to be when I grow up?" After all, this wasn't about what other people thought I *should* do or be; this was about what *I wanted to do – and be!* Maybe I hadn't yet discovered the real ingredients to living my passion because I hadn't clearly defined what that passion was.

One thing I knew for sure was that my husband had taken early retirement six months before my last layoff, and if I was going to support our household in the manner to which he was accustomed, I had better get cracking on something!

A wise person once said, "If you love what you're doing, what you're doing will return the favor." Since I had always loved speaking, why not embark on a speaking career? My husband and I looked at the pros and cons of starting my own business and decided it was now or never. What I didn't realize at the time was that my transition was to be multidimensional.

In 2001, I had no sooner started some networking activities – trying to get a handle on how to turn my speaking and coaching skills into income – when I was derailed by hip replacement surgery. If that wasn't enough trauma, my mother became ill and passed away. So there I was, in the middle of a major career transition, trying to work through a health transition and the death of my beloved mother at the same time. As John Lennon wrote in the song *Beautiful Boy*, "Life is what happens to you while you're busy making other plans!"

With the help and moral support of my husband, a fair amount of convalescence, and intensive reflection on my part, I was at long last able to give my newfound passion the undivided attention it deserved.

It was already May, 2002, and I needed cold, hard cash immediately. I decided to market myself under my newly-formed consulting firm as an expert medical marketer, promoting medical services for a local company on a part time basis. In the meantime, I also joined the National Speakers Association and a local Toastmasters Group to learn more of what I needed to know about professional speaking. Then someone suggested that if I were to be a successful speaker and coach, I needed to write and publish a book. So, I wrote and self-published a book entitled, *Laid Off? Don't' Stress! How to Get from Mad to Glad*, which became a best-seller in 2006 and was later picked up and promoted by CNN in 2008. Who would have expected that?

I now consult and coach people on how to be their own best PAL—find their Passion, find their Acceptance of life situations, and find out how to Laugh. I also still work productively as a healthcare specialist, marketing various medical services for clinics and doctors.

Obviously, these multiple transitional journeys did not take place overnight. They were fraught with one challenge and detour after another. I had to dig down deep, dredging up every bit of faith and courage I could find to step out of my comfort zone and into the twilight zone of personal transformation. The day I was able to take that leap of faith, I found I was still harboring a good deal of insecurity and self-doubt. But because I was committed and accepted the challenge, that day was actually the beginning of a new, exciting, seven-year journey of learning to expect the unexpected in my life—and to welcome it.

Today I am a certified career coach, and I love helping others to discover, define, clarify and pursue their own passion. I have also found that I can not only survive as a speaker and coach, but I am also able to keep my husband in the manner to which he is accustomed!

* * * * *

Kitty Wiemelt founded Winds of Change Consulting, a coaching and consulting firm designed to touch the human spirit with levity and renewed perspective. She is the author of the best selling book, Laid Off? Don't Stress! How to Get from Mad to Glad. *Kitty is also co-author of* Seizing Your Success, *one of the volumes in the* Wake Up! Live the Life You Love *series, produced by Steven E. In addition, Kitty is currently a motivational speaker, a certified career coach, and a healthcare marketing specialist.*

Michael's Story

Three Words

A while ago I was driving along thinking of my daughter, which is quite easy for me to do these days, as I haven't seen her in a while. I miss her, as she is quite far away. I was recalling some of the times we spent together, especially when she was young, and how my memories of those times are among the happiest keepsakes of my life.

Then, as if there was need for punishment, recrimination and penitence for such happiness, I felt myself engulfed by a huge wave of guilt and anguish for my self-centeredness during a time in my life when it seemed that every breath I took was drawn solely to strengthen and nurture my ego.

The memories were drowning me: past visions of shouting at, being demanding of, nagging at, and running roughshod over this beautiful daughter who had been entrusted to my care—who loved me, along with her mother, more than anyone else in her life. My heart filled with desperation, hopelessness and a deep yearning to be understood. With every atom of my being, I wanted to take back all of my daughter's tears, all the pain I had inflicted, all the heartache, disappointment and breaches of trust I had caused.

Silently, I told her that even during the worst of those times, I loved her so much more than life itself.

At that moment, as if he were standing next to me, I clearly heard my father say, "**So did I.**"

Stunned by what I had just heard, I felt a lifetime's worth of hatred, animosity, bitterness, disappointment, and white-hot anger vacate my heart.

Until that moment, I had not realized what a crushing burden I had been carrying around with me through most of my childhood and all my adult years.

My father, a man of overwhelming ego, was as controlling and demanding as a person can be—belittling, putting down, criticizing, bullying, threatening—an emotionally and physically abusive person. Such were my memories of him.

Finding a way to deal with this, especially after charting my own life's course, which happened only long after my father died, had always seemed futile. How do you balance the scales with a dead man? It felt like I was struggling, exhausted and furious, in an ocean whose angry waves were never, ever going to let me reach a peaceful shore.

But then, in an instant, the struggle was over. The next moment, and many, many more that followed, overflowed with joy, with apologies to my father for my hardness of heart, asking for forgiveness and sending him love in place of the anger that had almost consumed me whenever I thought of him. I wanted him to know how truly sorry I was for letting hatred block the love in my heart from going out to him.

His three words to me had been an amazing gift. Forgiving my father and myself freed me from years of unnecessary self-inflicted pain and guilt. I have asked my daughter for forgiveness, opening the door to a new and empowering relationship with her. It has become crystal clear to me that the purpose of my life is to learn to live, love and forgive in every moment, learning to share these gifts in unlimited measure with everyone—and most of all, with myself.

* * * * *

Michael Haradon has taken as his life's mission bringing the Universal Presence into every moment of his life. He lives in deep gratitude for all those whose loving kindness have helped him reach this point in his journey.

Bill's Story

Live For Today!

I began my career in the electronic engineering field and became involved in designing and servicing military radar systems in Germany. When the military contract expired, I was offered a position within the same company to service and manage large-scale business and scientific computer systems.

Always looking for new opportunities, I later accepted an offer to purchase and manage an automotive electronics business. I found this new endeavor both challenging and financially rewarding. Under my management and leadership the business began to generate a nice profit and started to expand.

Things were going well in my business and personal life when tragedy struck. That was the year my beautiful 11-year-old daughter lost her battle with Leukemia. Several months later, still heartbroken and despondent, I decided to make an effort to divert the mental anguish and intense pain of my daughter's loss by immersing my mind, body, and soul in yet another career change. I was already a pilot, an aircraft owner, and had always enjoyed a great love for flying and aircraft; so I chose the aviation field to devote myself to, knowing my own emotional and mental well-being depended on it.

I helped start a new sales distribution firm serving one of the largest general aviation aircraft manufacturing firms in the country. Two years into the business, I was recognized as the highest volume salesman in the company by personally selling more than 72 aircraft in a single year. However, when a Phoenix aviation company asked me to work for them directly and promised an attractive salary, as well as a generous commission schedule, I decided to leave the responsibility of owning and running a business to somebody else.

Unfortunately, after a short period, the new company decided to drop the salary. I reasoned that if I was going to risk straight commission, I might as well risk running my own firm again. So I resigned and started my own aircraft sales, brokerage, and charter firm.

For a good period of time my company flourished. I seemed to spend a lot of my "time" thinking about "yesterday" and worrying about "tomorrow," but I still enjoyed a great income, lived in a large, beautiful home and maintained a very comfortable lifestyle. However, during the fifth year of operation, business began to slack off. I started taking on tasks that I had previously delegated in an effort to conserve cash flow. It wasn't long before I was doing all the work in my business with no time to work on my business. I soon discovered my company's survival had become all-consuming and I had no time for anything else. At age 66, I found myself coming in early, staying late, and when I wasn't there, I spent the rest of my time justifying why I wasn't. I had no family time, no personal time, no life! My intuition was telling me it was time to "stop and take stock," but I wasn't listening.

As often happens in situations of this nature, the added stress of trying to do everything myself began to take its toll. I started waking up in the morning with abdominal pains. My body was trying to tell me something, but again I was too busy to listen to my own intuition. When I finally broke down and decided to get medical advice, the doctor told me I had waited too long and diagnosed me with a severe case of diverticulitis. The disease had progressed to the point that bowel perforation looked imminent and surgery was the only thing that might prolong my life.

Now I was finally aware, it was time for me to wake up and smell the roses. I locked the front door of my business, turned my back and walked away!

It's fascinating how things seem to fall into place when you finally become aware of your mortality. The day I was locking up my office, an old customer of mine stopped by and asked me if I would sell his aircraft. He had found another business opportunity and needed a leaner financial picture so he could focus on prospering his new venture. When I explained why I was no longer selling aircraft, he handed me some information regarding his new business and asked me to call him later.

In the meantime, since there was considerably more money going out of my household than coming in, I was forced to move out of my home into something more affordable and began focusing on getting healthy again. Then to my surprise, during one of my many doctor visits, I was told that my medical picture was improving and I would not require surgery after all. As my symptoms dissipated, I finally called my old customer back and became involved in his multi-level business opportunity. I discovered I could work at my own pace, and I liked the idea of helping myself by helping other people help themselves. With a little consistent effort, I began noticing a return on my investment. I was feeling good again, my energy level was back to normal, and I had a very positive sense of well-being. But this was not the end of my story!

It was a day just like any other. I decided to catch up on my "honey do" list when I started experiencing chest pains. They started in the morning, and by the middle of the afternoon I stubbornly decided to go to the hospital. I was there for two days while they conducted one test after another, with no definitive results. As a matter a fact, I was released with a clean bill of health and was told to visit my cardiologist for a second opinion. My doctor reviewed the test results and concurred with the diagnosis that I was "fit as a fiddle." If I wished, I was told the next step was a somewhat evasive, extensive and uncomfortable angiogram, and although the doctor applauded my penchant for certainty, he suggested that the test results didn't indicate the need for one. At that moment, my nagging intuition sent me a loud and clear message that couldn't be ignored. This prompted me to opt for the test.

While I lay on the gurney during the test, my intuitive powers were confirmed. I was informed that two of my major heart arteries were all but completely blocked. One was 75% closed, the other almost 95%. Cardiologists often refer to this type of double vessel blockage as the "widow maker." After several unsuccessful attempts to insert "stents" in the blocked arteries, it was decided that open heart surgery was the only option, and I underwent a double bypass.

My convalescence was nothing short of miraculous. I was home again in three days and back to my normal activities in no time. Today, I thoroughly enjoy the dynamics of my growing new business. I take time for my family and I try to live every day as if it were my last by focusing on what I'm doing, whom I'm doing it with, and why I am doing it at any given moment.

If I've learned anything through this litany of trans-formational experiences, it is that "there is just not enough time to lament about the past, or worry about the future, when there's a life to be lived today!"

* * * * *

Bill Festa currently conducts his business in Arizona, where he makes the most of every day, experiencing all that life has to offer, loving and living with his family.

Sonia's Story

From Making a Living to Making a Life

For as long as I can remember, I have lived a very ambitious and highly motivated life. I broke ground on my corporate career experience shortly after I earned my first Masters degree in Industrial and Organizational Psychology by beginning as the manager of an outbound market research call center for a medically-oriented monthly magazine.

After two and half years with the magazine, I moved into management for a major human resources consulting firm in the Big Apple (New York City), a position I thoroughly enjoyed. Next, I managed the human resources department of a publishing company, where I soon found the day-to-day grind of operational management tedious and completely uninspiring.

I decided that a major change was needed, so I moved to Phoenix and took time off to return to business school and refresh and expand my educational credentials. When I finished school, I accepted a position with a bank in a rotational leadership development program that eventually evolved into a project management role. This allowed me to finally get comfortable with what I thought might just be the long-term career opportunity I was seeking. Just as I began to feel that I was truly moving forward, bank policy changed, a number of people were let go, and I was unceremoniously laid off!

I started wondering if the idea of having a so-called "secure monthly salary" was really security after all. Although I had tried a few entrepreneurial endeavors in the past, I had basically opted for a regular paycheck. But now my earlier thoughts about how to make a living were finally beginning to change.

I didn't realize I was already in a transition until I was offered what appeared to be a promising position with a rapidly growing company. I took one look at the cubicle I would be working in and made a decision, right then and there, never to return to "cube land" again. That was the moment when I decided it was time to stop making a living and start making a life!

Since my husband and I had attended business school together and had both earned MBA degrees, we already knew how team-oriented we were and began to recognize that the mental synchronicity and compatibility we had developed together in the academic environment might serve us well in the world of practical work. So, we pooled our creative resources and applied our combined abilities to a common goal. With my qualifications in project management and my keen understanding that customer experience is king, I decided to create a company of my own! My aspirations were to assist companies with revenue generation by implementing and adapting concepts my husband and I had acquired. We developed systems that we believed would produce a substantially improved customer experience for our clients' customers.

It was slow going at first, but little by little we began building a significant customer base and demonstrating convincingly that our methods worked. However, we had tapped out our home equity line of credit, maxed out our credit cards, and were starting to eye ball our IRA accounts. It took 13 months of networking and building strong relationships to create a solid reputation, but perseverance paid off, and eventually we were rewarded with referrals on a consistent basis.

The one ingredient that made the most transformational difference in our life was the shift in our mindset—away from "working for" and toward "working on." There's nothing wrong with holding down a good job, but "working on" your own dreams and aspirations, instead of just "working for" someone else's, offers the biggest and most satisfying payoff of all!

* * * * *

Sonia Graham is Chief Experience Officer of Maximum Business Advantage, the Customer Experience Experts, located in Phoenix, Arizona.

Paul's Story

Big Boys Don't Cry!

St. Patrick's Day, March 17, 1971. That was the day I got "snipped" — had a vasectomy. My wife and I had discussed it many times. We had five children. One of them, Kendra, a heart patient who had been born with several deformities, was seven years old at that time and doing quite well. One by one the defects were being corrected surgically, but we knew that no matter what happened, we shouldn't have any more children. "Snipping" was our answer.

April 4, 1971, Kendra died in the hospital after complications from an elective surgery.

Have I told you that vasectomy isn't a reversible procedure? At least it wasn't then. So with her passing, we not only lost a child but also had forfeited the ability to have another.

I didn't know which terrible event to grieve over more: the loss of a daughter or my loss of male reproductive power. In fact, try as I might, I couldn't grieve at all — over anything. Perhaps it was my male conditioning, my need to "hold up under pressure," but I repressed all grief (and, I suspect, sublimated a lot of guilt), and this condition lasted for many years.

Fast-forward to the spring of 1990. Married life hadn't gone well after Kendra's death. We tried, we really did. I had long since stopped drinking and smoking, had trained as a financial planner, and opened a practice of my own that was relatively successful. But my wife did nothing but grieve, while I couldn't grieve at all. We understood each other less and less over time, and the feelings of isolation grew with each passing day. Finally, the marriage broke apart one Saturday night, and Sunday morning I left home, found a room to rent, moved out — and began a descent into a hell of depression.

The next couple of years, saw the biggest transition in my life and would lead to a transformation of greater depth and significance than I ever could have imagined. But on that Sunday, as I undressed for bed alone in an unfamiliar room that reeked of the residual odor of the bacon that my landlady had been frying earlier in the evening, I began a serious monologue about why and how I should kill myself.

Do you believe in angels? I don't. And no angel appeared to me that night. But I managed to survive, and even to get a couple of hours of sleep. The next day, a good friend — an angel? — called me quite early in the morning, sensed the despair in my tone of voice, and spent several hours counseling me and directing me to therapy, which I had resisted many times during the bad times in my marriage.

In rapid succession, I sold my financial planning practice, took a no-brainer job so I could concentrate on myself rather than worry about everyone else's problems, began attending a new church (well, actually, I hadn't attended church in a very long time, but my daughter introduced me to a way of thinking [and living] called New Thought), and gradually my life began to simplify, clarify, intensify — and transform!

Yes, it took two years to realize the transformation, and there were lots of little and big transitions — from job to job, discipline to discipline, growth opportunity to growth opportunity. But by 1995, I was a different, better and happier person than I had ever been. I had recognized, expressed and released all the grief over the losses of daughter, marriage and self. Because I had finally learned to grieve, I had worked my way through the depression to a freedom that has remained with me ever since.

I don't know what tomorrow holds, but whatever it may be, I welcome it, look forward to it, and know, as Dr. Reinhold Neibuhr has written, that my remaining days on this planet will be spent "living one day at a time, enjoying one moment at a time, accepting hardship as the pathway to peace . . ."

I know this because I've been through it all.

* * * * *

Beverly's Story

The Diagnosis!

For the last 24 years I have been a practicing Buddhist. As part of my daily ritual, I chant, "Nam Myoho Renge Kyo," which is a form of verbal meditation. I mention this because I attend biweekly group discussions at my local Buddhist cultural center, and in mid-August of 2007, I began to notice that every time I attended a different discussion group, the subject matter seemed to center around a single theme — "courage." I found this a curious phenomenon, since our discussions have always been varied and generally have covered a broad range of interesting and thought-provoking subjects.

It took another month of living with this awareness before I discovered the reason behind this message of courage. In late September of 2007, I kept my standing yearly mammogram appointment and was advised I may have breast cancer. I felt paralyzed as fear and disbelief proceeded to affect my ability to listen to and understand the reality of the attending physician's words. I immediately contacted a friend of mine, a doctor who specialized in radiation oncology. She conferred with the doctor at the mammogram center and then lovingly and patiently interpreted the diagnosis for me. After a follow-up biopsy confirmed a malignancy, I finally realized the gravity of my situation. I needed surgery. If, during the lumpectomy, they found that the cancer had spread, the prognosis could be grim indeed.

Although the surgery was inevitable, I decided I was going to do everything in my power to meet this challenge head-on prior to the procedure. The first thing I did was to significantly increase the frequency of my daily Diamoku (chanting) and meditation. In addition, I began drinking massive amounts of juice. I kept my mind focused, positive and relaxed, and I also tried to listen to what my body was telling me. I suddenly felt so alive! Life had such a profound meaning to me now, to the point that I had no concept of yesterday or tomorrow. Only the present moment seemed to matter to me.

When I visited the surgeon's office a few weeks later for my pre-surgery exam, the doctor was astonished to discover that the cancer had shrunk by almost 20%. Thinking it better to err on the side of caution, he performed the lumpectomy on November 18th and followed up with localized radiation for good measure. That was it! There was no need for further treatment, and I have remained cancer free.

While going through this two-month transition, I admit I was initially overwhelmed with uncertainty and just plain scared stiff. But as I continued to embrace my divine presence and listen to the messages my body was sending, I maintained an incredibly healthy body—no downtime and no malaise or nausea. I enjoyed an unusually high level of energy, experienced very little physical discomfort, and despite my diagnosis, also began to disengage myself from the drama and was again able to feel at peace with myself.

This transforming experience has literally changed my life and the way I think. Prior to the diagnosis and the events that followed, I had been so focused and busy thinking about my future goals and aspirations, I forgot to live my life today. I now take the time to stop and smell the roses; and I find that the way I interact and treat people not only serves me, but them as well.

I was missing out on the important things in life, such as friends, family, and taking the time to assist others who haven't been as fortunate as me. The abundance of overflowing joy in my heart routinely brings tears to my eyes and fills every aspect of my life. I know now this was a very necessary experience, and it was absolutely instrumental in helping me wake up to my full potential as a human being. I could have very well stayed asleep for the rest of my life, never to have known the joy and love I feel today. I can see clearly now, and I feel so very much alive!

* * * * *

Beverly P. is a practicing member of Soka Gakkai International - USA Buddhist and an Independent Product Consultant for a network marketing firm.

Ray's Story

Living by Accident to Living on Purpose

Floating.

That is the only way I can describe the first 40 years of my existence. I have always leaned toward being spiritual, rather than religious. Dogma did not dictate my actions. There was no point. Life was random, happenstance, a freak accident that placed me where I was and with whomever I was with.

When I was in my 20s, I believed that people over 40 were "old," that they didn't enjoy their lives, that they were serious and without joy. I was certain I didn't want that for my future. Therefore, I didn't live as though the future had anything to offer me. I didn't plan; I was a zombie going through my days on automatic pilot, unaware, unconscious, living by accident, using up precious oxygen.

Up until my marriage, my relationships followed a simple pattern:

1. Find a wounded partner.
2. Do what I could to wash those wounds.
3. Hope to have my needs fulfilled (love, sex, happiness, etc.).
4. Feel anxious and disappointed that my "fixing" didn't get me what I wanted.
5. Rinse.
6. Repeat.

I set myself up for failure and didn't even know it. I assumed I knew what my partner needed or wanted. I then expected that, once I fulfilled their assumed needs or wants, they would, in turn, fulfill my needs and wants. I grew up believing in this system, this "tit for tat" arrangement, that treated love as a consequence of my "good" actions.

At the age of 28, I married my wife to end this cycle. My new story was that I had to focus on giving all my attention to my marriage. Therefore, I closed myself off from the things I loved (friends, personal interests, etc.) to be what I thought my wife wanted me to be. If I was everything to her—friend, companion, lover, parent—I believed I would finally receive the love I desired.

My 40th birthday changed everything. I wanted the kind of birthday celebration I had given my wife on her 40th birthday, two years prior. I expected a party at a nice restaurant, with 10 to 15 of my closest friends, in a huge celebratory recognition of my reaching a milestone. My birthday ended up being a simple dinner outing with my parents, wife, and kids at a restaurant I didn't choose, topped off by bad-tasting food. It felt like it could have been any other day. There I was, 40, profoundly disappointed that no one recognized me. I suddenly realized that it was up to *me* to give myself what I expected others to give me.

Soon after my 40th birthday, one of my IT clients introduced me to the world of inner exploration. This marked the point at which the weave of my married life started to unravel. My path became one of self-discovery. I focused on books, movies, seminars, anything that would get me closer to understanding myself. In my self-exploration, I shared my discoveries with my wife. Instead of encouragement and validation, she shut me down. I then began to push away from my marriage. In response, my wife's normal yelling became louder, her anger fiercer, her sarcasm sharper. Consequently, I turned toward sharing my growth experiences with my IT client, who was also married, finding the validation and encouragement I was deeply wanting from my wife. My IT client became my lover, someone who shared my personal discoveries with me.

By turning my attention inward, I distanced myself from the rules I had set up and lived by for the past 11 years. For instance, previously my wife had made all the decisions on raising the children and the friendships she and I were allowed. We were together 24/7, with only her friends around. Now, I began taking an active stance about how the children should be raised, voicing my opinions, as well as growing my circle of friends and experiences.

The stress of continuing the affair, not wanting to give up my sole source of acknowledgment and validation, took a physical toll. My heart hurt for months on end. To help the pain I turned to psychotherapy, alcohol and anti-depressants. I went from being the obedient husband to the antichrist. However, once I finally surrendered to the pain and accepted responsibility, the layers of my former self slowly began peeling away, revealing a side of me I didn't know existed. Instead of relating to people as a means to an end and loving on a conditional basis, I began to make heartfelt connections, listening to what people were feeling, and loving as a gift, not a bartering chip.

Through this life transition from husband to divorcée, I've learned many lessons. I made up a lot of disempowering agreements about who I was supposed to be and how I was to conduct myself as a husband and father. Having an affair lacked integrity and was dishonoring to my wife, to my kids, to my marriage, and to myself. By choosing to break my word through having the affair and leaving the marriage, much pain was brought upon my family and ultimately upon myself. I modeled poor behavior for our children. I showed my son that it was acceptable for men to cheat and disrespect women—that women deserved to be treated as disposable. I showed my daughter to expect and accept disrespect from men—that women are not worthy of fidelity and honor. In hindsight, with the tools and training I have acquired since the divorce, reflecting upon the decision, I would choose not to divorce. My lack of integrity and lack of awareness as to the repercussions of my choices and my disregard for those I loved was the problem, not the marriage.

I have come to realize that I create the life that I want. I am responsible for my happiness. I am complete and whole, and my life partner is the bonus in life that makes it all worth sharing. I am an honorable man of integrity, with a profound respect for women—the kind of man that I wish my son to grow up to be and the kind I wish for my daughter. I support my ex-wife in the raising of our children and I remain a strong presence in their lives. If a similar situation came up again, I would acknowledge the urge to run away and push to discover how I could make the situation work for my partner and myself, with integrity and love.

Shifting from living by accident to living on purpose was a shift from living in reaction to living with intention. Destroying my marriage, losing my wife and my kids, instilled within me integrity and responsibility by showing me the ripple effect of my actions and how immediate gratification affects more than just myself. Through this loss and introspection, I came to know my true purpose, my empowering connections. Now my personal as well as business life is centered around my commitment to assisting others in identifying the blocks that tend to stop people from discovering their passion and purpose in life. For this, I am eternally grateful.

* * * * *

Ray Barber: Chi Solutions, Inc.
info@chisolutions.com
http://empoweredconnections.wordpress.com

Marty's Story

You Won't Miss It Until It's Gone

Places do not die as people do, but over time they often change so fundamentally that little is left of what they once were. The landscape that spreads over a part of my country, Cuba, is timeless, but the land I remember today is a Cuba of several pasts.

The house I lived in until I was nine years old was located on a narrow street lined with large trees. I recall sitting on the steps in the afternoons as warm breezes rustled the leaves. I have no story from that neighborhood or that house; in fact, I have only disconnected bits of memory. Though memories of my life there are few and flawed, I think often of one fragment: my parents' constant love and hard work, which kept the family together and our American Dream alive.

Our family crest reads: Courageous & Unified to overcome all odds. My family has had to come together and be courageous in order to stand up for what we believe. I am a stronger person today because of my family's determination never to give up on their dreams.

When Fidel Castro became the prime minister in the late 1950s, thousands of Cubans — including my father — disapproved of Communism and rebelled against the government. This group of anti-communist activists tried desperately to force Castro out of power. In 1960, my father, one of the leaders of this underground group, secretly met with several other leaders across the island to plan strategies for dissolving the Communist government.

In 1961, despite his love for Cuba, my father decided he loved his family more and knew he did not want to subject my mother, my sister, and me to Communism. Therefore, he began to make plans to leave the country legally. When he discussed this with other leaders of the underground, they felt betrayed and became angry. Frustration overcame reason, and they eventually turned on him, and a warrant was issued for his arrest. He found out about this and went into hiding, using this time to plan our exodus from Cuba.

Meanwhile, my mother, sister and I had to survive without a father. We were followed everywhere we went. Our home was watched by government officers 24 hours a day. We told them my father fled the country and that he had left us behind.

For a full year we had no idea where he really was, and that was actually fortunate because we feared coercion and believed that torture might even be used by the government to obtain information from us. Since I was a little girl without her father and could never be sure about his welfare, I became somewhat despondent and withdrawn, wondering if I would ever see him again.

Early February, 1963, we were told of my father's plans to escape. The plan was that we were to attend a baptism party in early March at the home of a family that was also planning to escape the island. They were part of a movement that had been formed to help families throughout the country escape the tyranny of Communism by sailing to the United States.

We were told to bring to the party everything we wanted to take with us for the escape. In essence, our only real luggage was *hope!* I remember collecting only enough things that would fit into a single bag, and then off we went to the party.

Since my mom's mother had passed away when she was a child, she was raised by her grandmother. I recall my mom saying goodbye to her grandmother without ever telling her about our escape plan for fear that the government would come and torture her for information. To this day, my mom holds a vivid memory of her grandmother waving goodbye as tears filled my mother's eyes because she knew that this would be the last time she would see her. As for me, I grew up not ever really knowing my great grandmother.

When we arrived at the party, we didn't recognize my dad; he had disguised himself so as to blend in with the hundreds of guests and not be identifiable as one of the leaders of the underground movement. He told my mom that 21 of us were leaving that night in a 21-foot rowboat. When the last guests left the party late that night, my family and the others who had decided to escape were driven in a small convoy of automobiles to a farm many miles away. On arrival, we were tersely instructed, "Get out!" Anxious and desperate, we watched as the cars sped away into the night, leaving us alone and afraid. Adjacent to the farm, there was a small market, where we waited for the next phase of our journey to begin. An hour later, a cracker truck pulled up in back of the store and pretended to deliver crackers while all 21 of us were quietly but quickly loaded into the vehicle.

My memories of that truck and that night were permanently etched into the deepest recesses of my impressionable young mind. I remember looking inside the truck as I was being lifted into it and noticing that everyone was struck silent with fear. I, too, was absolutely terrified. Once inside the truck, we were taken to a seaside location where a government fishing boat was docked. The men in our party were told to carry gasoline cans out of the truck. But because the truck driver feared being caught, he gave the men just enough time to unload the gasoline before hurriedly departing. As a result, our food, medicine, and most of our personal belongings were left behind, including the birth certificates, clothing and water.

Shortly after that, we were told we couldn't depart that evening due to bad weather. However, we could travel four miles down shore to a less rocky area, where another boat would meet us, and we could leave from there. Having no alternative, all 21 of us walked slowly and quietly down the shoreline, across beaches, through marshes, and into and out of swamps so as not to be discovered. As we crawled under one of several fences we encountered, I remember seeing some horses in the distance and appreciating their beauty. I tried to get my mother's attention, but she was too immersed in her prayers.

Finally, two hours later, we made it to the shore, where a tiny wooden boat was waiting to carry us 90 long miles to Florida.

As we began our journey over water, we lay back on each other's laps so we wouldn't be seen by the Cuban military. One man, the government fisherman, sat up and pretended to be fishing until we left Cuban waters. Once we made it out of Cuban waters, we were able to run the motor without fear of being heard. After about four hours of bouncing around in the rolling seas, we were finally greeted by the morning sun. We smiled when we saw seagulls, thinking we must be close to land. However, our joy was short-lived when we realized the seagulls were trying to outrun a violent tropical storm.

I remember the storm produced huge waves that almost shredded our tiny boat. We were drenched and nearly thrown overboard with each crash of the waves. We were tossed around so much that our helmsman lost his bearings and headed deeper into the Gulf of Mexico, away from the safety of our Florida destination. I remember my mom praying aloud, and—one by one—we all joined in, continuing to pray for our lives until finally, two long hours later, our prayers were answered when a U.S. nuclear submarine in the Gulf of Mexico spotted us and alerted a Navy destroyer in the area to pick us up.

When our rescue vessel arrived, the sailors who helped us aboard found us to be a group of hungry and exhausted voyagers. We were wet and sunburned, with our skin rubbed raw from the salt water. I remember our tiny boat crashing against the destroyer with every wave as we were being pulled to safety by ropes and ladders. My father was the last one off the fishing boat. As he was lifted onto the destroyer's deck, one final crashing wave hurled the fragile wooden boat against the side of the Navy vessel, where it split into hundreds of pieces.

Once aboard the destroyer, we were taken to a warm, comfortable galley to be fed, or to a dispensary for medical treatment as needed, and soon we were transferred to a Coast Guard patrol boat for the final leg of our trip.

When we arrived in Key West, Florida, my dad stepped off the boat, immediately dropped to his knees, and kissed the ground. At that moment our lives were transformed. We were free at last!

Next—and finally—we were sent to Miami, where the Immigration Office processed us for admittance to the land of our dreams, America.

Sometimes it's hard to explain to others the joyous, heartfelt elation of being free, especially when they have never lived without freedom. To those like my family, who endured so much just to live in freedom, the United States of America is truly a gift from God.

None of us has been able to go back to live in Cuba since the escape; but in 2008, my son Stephen had the opportunity to visit Cuba to attend a media conference. When he returned, he shared with me how the Cuban people seem to be naturally happy even though they don't have the best living conditions. He reported that they have one thing: they continue to live with the hope and dream that their beloved country will one day be free and prosperous again.

During my son's stay, he was able to visit the house I grew up in and took some photos. What wonderful memories he brought back to us!

As he was flying out of Havana he wrote these words;

> *As my American Airlines charter flight flew out of Havana over the sea, I couldn't help but think about you mom and the family's very same journey, but with a vastly different experience – paddling to the United States on a wooden raft, risking your lives for a taste of freedom. How incredible!*
>
> *Now, more than ever, I recognize the tremendous sacrifice the family made to leave Cuba, and my good fortune to be here. I believe more than ever that one must have dreams and go for what you truly desire in your life. Today, perhaps more than ever before, I am extremely proud and grateful to be Cuban-American.*

Although I was only a child, I had an experience that taught me the price individuals are willing to pay for freedom. I often wonder what might have happened if my family had given up on their dream. What would my life look like? Would I have been different? These questions still haunt me sometimes.

Yet I know I'm just making myself crazy with the "what ifs," and that my life has unfolded as it was meant to. I know I am living the life I am living today because my family has always kept the promise of freedom alive in their hearts. I know I am living proof that the freedom the American Dream promises exists. I also know that—not unlike freedom itself—if you don't take time to be grateful for each blessing, you won't miss it until it's gone!

* * * * *

Martha (Marty) Croissant, born in Havana, emigrated to the U.S. at the age of nine. Her life has been rich in both Cuban and American traditions. Marty and her husband, Rick, have operated their own successful network marketing business since 2005 in Tucson, Arizona. Network marketing has given them the opportunity to inspire thousands of people to achieve remarkable success and to truly live the American Dream of entrepreneurship and time-freedom.

Marty is presently at work on her first book, which is about her family's courageous escape from Communism, and their heroic story of drifting at sea for the freedom that the American Dream promises. This story is an abridged excerpt from her forthcoming book.

EPILOGUE

Yesterday is already a Dream,
and Tomorrow is only a Vision
but every Today, well lived,
makes every Yesterday
a Dream of Happiness
and every Tomorrow
a Vision of Hope.

~ from the Sanskrit

This book isn't intended to highlight any one person's life; rather, it is meant to serve as an example and to help people from all walks of life facilitate their transformational journeys.

My story is little more than a testament to a lifetime of trial and error. I have spent a good deal of my time on Earth subscribing to and studying personal development gurus, attending seminars, and analyzing soul-searching texts in an effort to capture the ever-elusive holy grail of joy and peace of mind.

I began to realize that many of the sages of the ages were more alike than not, and their message unnervingly familiar. As my mind opened, my search eventually evolved into a heartfelt exploration and settled into an experience instead of a means to an end.

Deciding what I was going to trade the rest of my days for was far from being my first transition, and it won't be the last; but it was, nonetheless, the nearest and dearest to my heart. I truly found *myself* in this latest process, and have discovered a good deal about my past—and the present consequences of unresolved emotions from my childhood.

The very act of researching and developing this book has provided an insight and understanding regarding my own life that I might have never realized otherwise. It has allowed me to break free of old, disempowering beliefs and move on to a new and exciting chapter in my story. It was like finding the long-lost pieces of an unsolved puzzle.

This experience gave me the clarity, confidence and passion I needed to move forward with *Tucker Tales*, my value-based children's book series. This life-changing, transformational process has helped me create a new and exciting self-directed destiny. Not only have I been able to manifest a vehicle with *Tucker Tales* that is designed to help children deal with the trials, tribulations, and everyday emotions of growing up, but I have also been blessed with the book you are reading right now, which I hope will serve as a guide to coach and assist adults of all ages with the ongoing challenges of transition.

The principles and methods expressed in this book, which are both ancient and contemporary, seem to touch the very core of the human condition. Although I had no hand in their creation, I can happily say that I am a satisfied recipient of their ageless wisdom. I believe that people, regardless of present circumstances or history, can successfully transcend their former life and achieve a new beginning by following some of the basic principles in this text.

They must, however, be willing to take a mental "time out" to reintroduce themselves to their authentic self and let go of all those disempowering and limiting beliefs from the past. Life can be wondrous, or it can be reduced to something that falls far short of our expectations.

What we expect can and does facilitate what we see and attract. However, the core principle here is not so much what we expect; rather, it is how we perceive what we have observed. When we expect our interpretations of past observations to be true, we have a tendency to blindly accept that truth as our reality now. It's only later, sometimes much later, we realize that our truth was only as good as our personal perspective during some past event. When we try to adapt this perceived truth to the present, we are often surprised to find it no longer applies, and we again find ourselves in a state of transition.

* * * * *

The butterfly of happiness remains elusive
only if we continue to chase it.
It is only when we are quiet and true to our heart
that we are able to spread our wings
and soar toward new horizons!

~ Jamie Wagner

Sending You Love and Joy,

Jamie

A GLOSSARY OF TERMS
AS USED IN THIS BOOK

I trust that the terms as presented in this glossary will assist in your enjoyment of this book, with the understanding that the definitions I've used within these pages may or may not be synonymous with traditional definitions. Since we all come from varied backgrounds, we sometimes hear and see things differently. Therefore, accepted meanings for many commonly used words sometimes change, depending upon their application and diverse cultural inclinations. Thank you for refraining from strict adherence to any single definition and for taking the time necessary to consider the intent behind the usage. Enjoy!

* * * * *

Acceptance
affirmation; confirmation; abidance by; compliance with; embracing of

Affirmation
a statement written and verbalized, with heartfelt feeling, in the present tense, to assist with the transformation of a belief into a knowing and eventually a physical reality

Allowing
making room to accept an idea, thought or a new reality by removing all doubt, thus surrendering all resistance

Ambivalence
uncertainty between two possible choices; indecisiveness; inability to make a decision based on two opposing thoughts about the same subject

Attention
a conscious awareness and focus; as attending to our intent

Attitude
personal demeanor; a frame of mind with which one approaches one's life and ultimately directs one's behavior

Authentic Self
expression of your true self; that which is not drama-driven ego

Awareness
being completely conscious and present in "real time"; being in the "now"

Belief
an intellectual conceptualization that develops into repetitive thought, becomes a habit and evolves into a preconceived notion, which may or may not have a basis in truth

Butterfly
a powerful mythical symbol of change, joy, light and transformation

Cause
that from which all effects manifest; that which comes first; first cause always means that from which everything comes

Certainty
perceived truth; reality; knowing; trust; faith

Change
transition/transformation; to let go of the old and to experience the new

Clarity
conscious awareness; focus; inner understanding; as opposed to scattered thinking

Clock Time
a measuring device supported by the use of the clock and calendar used to schedule one's life and or guide one's perceived physical reality

Coach
one who mentors, guides, motivates, supports, encourages, listens and asks questions in an effort to help one excel through the sharing of various personal development techniques; special coaching categories may include personal development, transition/transformation, lifestyle, health, inner personal relationships, business operations, sales and marketing techniques

Coincidence
most commonly defined as an unpredictable event or incidental occurrence as in serendipity; also defined as a very predictable synchronicity as in an instance of coinciding

Commitment
giving one's word to one's self; to decide with clarity and confidence

Compassion
expression of empathetic concern for others; a state of knowing and understanding; being sensitive to others needs and feelings

Conscious
awake; alert; self aware; knowing; on purpose; in the "now," to be more than present; to be with the presence

Cocoon
a metaphor for metamorphosis; the transformation stage or gap between an ending and a beginning; a time-out for reflection, re-evaluation and reorganization

Dance
a metaphor for taking action in your life through the heartfelt, all knowing, creative consciousness; living life

Decision
resolve; a determined commitment of mind

Divine Guidance/Divine Intervention
an all knowing universal creative and spiritual consciousness that exists to assist in the manifestation of physical reality

Dream
a vision; an aspiration; an imagined event; to fantasize

Dream Stealers
family members, friends or business associates that may or may not have good intentions but lack the information, vision and purpose to give appropriate advice

Effect
that which follows cause; the manifestation of that which is the procuring cause

Ego
that part of your being that you mentally conceptualize as being you; most often a sociological perception of misidentification

Emotional Feelings
born of intellectual concepts and ideas; feelings developed from the perceptions of past and current events usually resulting in some form of active behavior; mental energy set in motion

Energy
that which can neither be created nor destroyed; that which always is and the source of all there is or ever will be; sometimes referred to as life itself, Spirit or the Divine

Enthusiasm
the God within; excitement; passion; spirit

Explore
the act of finding something you already have; discovery

Faith
an inner knowing that supports a heartfelt truth that cannot be denied; an experience as opposed to an intellectual concept; the substance hoped for, the evidence of things yet to be seen

Fear
false evidence appearing real; in opposition to faith; anticipation of pain

Feelings
see **Emotional Feelings** and **Heartfelt Feeling**

Forgiveness
to accept the event and embrace the pain; the act of releasing blame or guilt and setting yourself free

Freedom
independence; ability to choose; self direction; to express life as one personally desires

Giving
to contribute; to donate; to serve unconditionally

Giving Up
lose hope; call it quits; abandon; choosing to lose

Goal
a purpose; intention; aspiration; destination

Grace
a gift from the divine consciousness; a complete state of conscious awareness; a moment in time that allows for reflection, contemplation, rediscovery and reevaluation; the law of perpetual good and freedom; never one of limitation; as in the grace of God

Gratitude
thanksgiving; appreciation; counting your blessings; recognizing the good and abundance in life

Gratitude Journal
a book used to regularly record experiences, events and relationships to acknowledge appreciation and give thanks

Happiness
an emotional feeling of high spirits, enjoyment and euphoria

Heartfelt Feeling
a spiritual experience; an unexplainable inner knowing; intuition, language of the heart, not of the intellect; that which creates the manifestation of form through the formless divine consciousness

Identification
labels of self; recognition of characters we play

Inner Child
the essence of who we are; that which we left behind; the core of our soul; the center of our being; the hope for our future

Inspiration
the awakening of the spirit within, through the use of, but not limited to; art, music, teachings, movies, literature and experiences, etc.

Intention
purpose; goal; aspiration; specific focus

Intuition
higher self; insight; a feeling; a hunch; that which is supported by an inner knowing; a divine insight; a sixth sense; an instinctive understanding; heartfelt feeling

Joy
pure pleasure; enjoyment; delight; excitement; high spirits; a state of being stimulated by the expectancy of perceived good

Judgment
a presupposition based on a preconceived notion

Knowing
true faith; an experiential understanding of truth; inner consciousness

Law of Attraction
a thought strengthened by intense emotion or a heartfelt feeling, which supports behavior consistent with that thought and ultimately manifests the unformed thought into form; we attract what we think and feel and through action manifest the results, good or bad, based on the nature of the original thought

Law of Gender
every seed has a gestation or incubation period

Listening
a method of understanding with the heart as opposed to hearing with one's ears

Manifest
to create; to show forth or to make evident

Mastermind
coordinating knowledge in a spirit of harmony, collectively between two or more people for the attainment of a definite purpose

Me
that which I am, yet cannot be described; the essence of all that I am that cannot be identified as such

Meditation
a method by which one may quiet ego based mind chatter, listen to the wisdom of the divine presence and co-create with the creative consciousness; listening to God

Miracle
a supernatural, mysterious or unexplainable event

Nature
that which comes unsynthesized from the universal source of all there is

Negative Emotions
feelings of fear, worry, doubt, regret, anger, grief, blame, resentment, boredom, hate, indecision, procrastination, ambivalence, indifference, guilt, jealousy, impatience, arrogance, revenge, depression, sadness, etc.

Passion
excitement; spirit; strong affection; hearts desire; inner motivation; enthusiasm

Patience
Law of Gender; all things manifest in their own good time; the art of waiting and persevering

Perception
seeing and interpreting something based on past thoughts, experiences, and personal perspectives

Perspective
view point; mental outlook; attitude; frame of mind

Personal Growth
expansion; a point from which we develop a perception of physical, intellectual or spiritual evolution

Positive Emotions
feelings of love, happiness, passion, enthusiasm, appreciation, freedom, gratitude, optimism, etc.

Prayer
a method of calling upon, summoning, co-creating and comunicating with the divine universal creative source; talking to God

Presence
life; being; spirit; divine consciousness

Present
experiencing and being consciously aware of what is happening right now during this moment; being in the "now"

Purpose

driving force; motivation; meaning; dream; vision; desire; reason; determination with incentive

Reaction

resistance; a reflex action based on fear as opposed to an appropriate response based on awareness; the law of cause and effect; an action induced by vital resistance to some other action

Real Time

an experiential understanding of the present as opposed to a clock and calendar perception of our physical reality; living in the "now"

Receiving

to gain from; obtain; embody; embrace or accept with reverence, respect, and gratitude

Regrets

current thoughts of past perceptions defined as mismanaged or unmanaged events, often manifesting grief, self punishment and frustration

Resistance

to react; to resist against; to be in opposition of; to fight against something as opposed to standing up for something

Response

an appropriate action supported by conscious awareness as opposed to a reflex reaction motivated by fear

Risk

uncertainty; danger; unpredictability; long shot; gamble; chance; to tempt a perceived fate

Sages

teachers with wisdom to share; prophets; mystics; philosopher; wise person; mentor; spiritual intuitive

Searching

looking for something you believe you don't have; to seek

Seeing

a method of heartfelt intuitive perception as opposed to looking at a perceived reality using your eyes only

Self Love

inner confidence; self respect; positive and empowering self image; compassion and reverence for one's own existence

Service

contribution; service to others; random acts of kindness; that which we give voluntarily or trade for economic function

Spirit

breath of life; soul; presence; motivating force; truth; God; Divinity; creative consciousness; the Universal I AM

Subconscious Mind

a place beneath the level of full consciousness where habits, pre-programmed charges or beliefs may reside

Success
the progressive realization of a worthy ideal; the journey

Surrender
letting go and letting God; the process of giving in but not giving up; the art of allowing intuition as opposed to forcing ideas and intellectual reason

Thoughts
that which one mentally conceptualizes; to think; an intellectual activity

Transition
transforming one's perceptions and initiating a new beginning; an experiential journey of letting go of past encumbrances; the passage from one psychological or physical state to another

Transformation
the process of changing ones thought patterns, perceptions and paradigms in an effort to successfully navigate a transition; the cocoon stage of any metamorphosis

Truth — Authentic
supported by faith; a deep, heartfelt knowing; an experience as opposed to an intellectual concept; real truth is changeless and complete within itself

Uncertainty
ambivalence; doubt; confusion; lack of confidence

Unconditional Love
absolute; unrestricted love given freely without judgments or conditions

Unconscious
"the lights are on, but nobody's home"; oblivious; unaware; unknowing; spiritually asleep

Vision
seeing that which has yet to be manifested

Vision Board
also commonly referred to as vision album or treasure map; a powerful visual tool that assists in manifesting goals, dreams, and desires

Visualization
seeing with the heart; to envision through the mind's eye, a desired reality

FAITH

Faith can move mountains,
no matter how steep,
and calm the rough waters,
no matter how deep.

Faith can change darkness
to heavenly light,
while leading us tranquilly
out of the night.

All this I can grant, with
assurance, you see,
for countless are the mountains
Faith has moved for me.

~ Laura Baker Haynes

JUST LIKE A CHILD

Song lyrics*

Just like a child, every day's new.
I've got nothing to hide and nothing to prove.
I'm living on purpose, with joy in my soul
To be happy and peaceful, perfect and whole…
Like a child.

I'm going to paint and draw to my heart's content
And dress in fancy clothes
I'm going to make a wish and toss the coin
And dream for hours on end!

With a plastic crown and a flowery sheet
I'm going to be a king or a queen!
I'm going to run as fast as I possibly can
And love unconditionally!

I'm going to play until the sun goes down
And dance like no one's watching!
I'm going to spread my arms like wings to fly
And sing a joyful song!

~ Jeanne Mac Laughlin and Barbara Horton

Lyrics from the song "Just Like A Child"

The JaJa's – Music to Live By. All Rights Reserved
Shift The Drift CD is available on line at *http://www.thejajas.com*

MEET THE AUTHORS

Jamie Wagner is devoted to helping adults help themselves as they journey through the anxiety and confusion associated with life-changing transitions.

Aspiring to have an active, positive impact on children, and recognizing that the challenges of transitions are not limited to adults, Jamie and her husband, Bill, have also launched an entire series of value-based children's books entitled *Tucker Tales*.

The Wagners, along with their dogs, have chalked up thousands of miles touring the United States in their RV motor coach. When they aren't traveling or actively promoting their books, they spend most of their time with their Pembroke Welsh Corgis, Taylor (right) and, of course, the infamous Tucker (left).

Jamie enjoys cooking, reading, gardening, traveling, and collecting and creating dog art, while Bill has a penchant for cars, boats, motorcycles, RVs, and aviation, as well as enjoying music and art. Their mutual passion is entertaining friends and family, along with spending time with engaging people who share a love of life's unlimited possibilities.

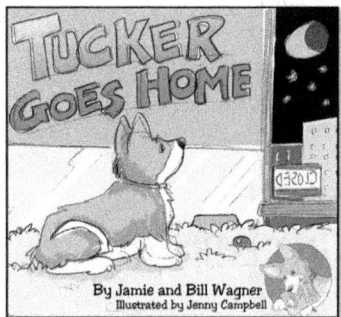

By Jamie and Bill Wagner
Illustrated by Jenny Campbell

Coming Soon!
TUCKER GOES HOME:
A Tale of Life, Love & Hope
Jamie and Bill Wagner
ISBN 978-0-9840585-1-6
Volume One
Tucker Goes Home is the first book in the Tucker Tales series of children's stories. It sets the stage for a lifetime of adventures for Tucker, an adopted, curious, mischievous and lovable Pembroke Welsh Corgi.

In this moving tale of wonder and uncertainty, you will follow Tucker as he longs for the love, the sense of belonging, and the security of a new home and family. Embrace Tucker's determination as he copes with adversity and strives to realize his hopes and dreams.

Ideal for reading to children as young as toddlers, this series of heartwarming tales provides parents, grandparents, and educators the opportunity to interact, connect and grow with children by sharing the basic values of life that all children should have the opportunity to learn and live by—during those impressionable early years!

For more information, visit Tucker at his website, *www.TuckerTaleProductions.com*

Throw your heart over the fence
and the rest will follow!

~ Norman Vincent Peale

A SPECIAL MESSAGE
AND A WORTHWHILE GIFT FOR YOU

You may be asking yourself, "Do these principles and methods really work?" The answer is: they do – if you apply them to your life and allow them to work for you.

We want our circumstances to change, but it's human nature to continue to think, believe and do things the same way. To effectively alter our life experience, we must change our thoughts, adjust our perceptions, and initiate alternative behavior that is consistent with our new insights.

What action plan will you implement for better results? Are you inspired about your new beginning, or has the daunting specter of the unknown filled your thoughts with worry and ambivalence? What can you do to disengage your focus from the "closing door," so that you can give your undivided attention to the new and exciting opportunities that are opening before you?

If you have decided to take full responsibility to change your life, move through your transition and choose a different path that meets your life's aspirations, I invite you to explore our various personal coaching programs and upcoming workshops that have been designed to help people to effectively navigate their transitions and accelerate the transformational process.

Just visit the website address on the next page. Click on the free gift icon and begin your journey now!

CLAIM YOUR FREE GIFT

Just a small token of our appreciation for the spirit in you and a symbol of our continued dedication to improving the quality of life individually and collectively.

Go to the website at *www.TuckerTaleProductions.com* and click on the **free gift icon.**

For personal coaching or workshop information, please contact **Coaching@TuckerTaleProductions.com** or **Workshops@TuckerTaleProductions.com**

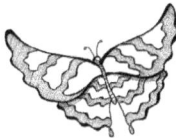

SHARE YOUR STORY!

Have you had a successful transitional journey you would like to share?

There are thousands of people in various stages of transition that would love to hear your story! Help us help them by telling your story and sharing your personal triumphs. Let your experiences be a conduit by which others might relate, giving them an opportunity to transform their lives, just as you have.

- Of all your life's challenges, what personal transitional experience made the greatest impact on your life—and why?
- What did you learn from your experience?
- Were you able to sense the impending transition?
- What made you decide it was time to stop and re-evaluate your life?
- What personal distinctions did you make that helped you close the door on the old so you could make room for the new?
- What perceptual changes did you have to make to break out of your cocoon and move on to a new beginning?
- Tell us more!

If you have a story to contribute and like the idea of possibly making a difference in someone else's life, let us know and we may select your "gift from the heart" for a future publication. We would love to hear from you. Please include your name and contact information, along with a 2- to 3-page outline of your story.

E-mail your story to:
ShareYourStory@TuckerTaleProductions.com

www.ingramcontent.com/pod-product-compliance
Lightning Source LLC
Chambersburg PA
CBHW052038090426
42739CB00010B/1954